ournemouth & poole

the college

This s   der-
gradu   ni   urces Centre and
perfor a   given
to produc   a   202 465 03   tance,
responding   at o: udy by the
work of   on   oo ry

The p   n is to present eac   al experience
in the mind of the reader – achie   y analysis of the
text in relation to its themes and theatricality. Emphasis is
accordingly placed on the relevance of the work to the
modern reader and the world of today. At the same time,
traditional views are presented and appraised, forming the
basis from which a creative response to the text can develop.

In each volume, Part One: *Text* discusses certain key
themes or problems, the reader being encouraged to gain a
stronger perception both of the inherent character of the
work and also of variations in interpreting it. Part Two:
Performance examines the ways in which these themes or
problems have been handled in modern productions, and
the approaches and techniques employed to enhance the
play's accessibility to modern audiences.

Synopses of the plays are given and reference is made to
the commentaries of critics and other writers on the texts and
performances. A concluding Reading List offers guidance to
the student's independent study of the work.

PUBLISHED

ROSENCRANTZ AND GUILDENSTERN ARE DEAD, JUMPERS and THE REAL THING

Text and Performance

ROBERT GORDON

MACMILLAN

For Edith and Godfrey

First published 1991

Published by
MACMILLAN EDUCATION LTD
Houndmills, Basingstoke, Hampshire RC21 2XS
and London
Companies and representatives
throughout the world

Phototypeset by Input Typesetting Ltd, London
Printed in Hong Kong

British Library Cataloguing in Publication Data
Gordon, Robert
  Rosencrantz and Guildenstern are dead, Jumpers and The real thing – (Text and performance).
  1. Drama in English. Stoppard, Tom, 1937–
  I. Title II. Series
  822.914
  ISBN 0–333–43777–2

CONTENTS

GENERAL EDITOR'S PREFACE

For many years a mutual suspicion existed between the theatre director and the literary critic of drama. Although in the first half of the century there were important exceptions, such was the rule. A radical change of attitude, however, has taken place over the last thirty years. Critics and directors now increasingly recognise the significance of each other's work and acknowledge their growing awareness of interdependence. Both interpret the same text, but do so according to their different situations and functions. Without the director, the designer and the actor, a play's existence is only partial. They revitalise the text with action, enabling the drama to live fully at each performance. The academic critic investigates the script to elucidate its textual problems, understand its conventions and discover how it operates. He may also propose his view of the work, expounding what he considers to be its significance.

Dramatic texts belong therefore to theatre and to literature. The aim of the 'Text and Performance' series is to achieve a fuller recognition of how both enhance our enjoyment of the play. Each volume follows the same basic pattern. Part One provides a critical introduction to the play under discussion, using the techniques and criteria of the literary critic in examining the manner in which the work operates through language, imagery and action. Part Two takes the enquiry further into the play's theatricality by focusing on selected productions of recent times so as to illustrate points of contrast and comparison in the interpretation of different directors and actors, and to demonstrate how the drama has worked on the modern stage. In this way the series seeks to provide a lively and informative introduction to major plays in their text and performance.

MICHAEL SCOTT

ACKNOWLEDGEMENTS

My grateful acknowledgements are due to Tom Stoppard and to Faber and Faber, London, for permission to quote from *Rosencrantz and Guildenstern Are Dead, Jumpers* and *The Real Thing* and to Faber and Faber for permission to reprint an extract from 'The Love Song of J. Alfred Prufrock' in T. S. Eliot's *Collected Poems 1909–1962*. I wish to express my gratitude to Enid Foster at the British Theatre Association and Sue Winter in the National Theatre Scripts Department for their kind assistance.

PART ONE: TEXT

Rosencrantz and Guildenstern Are Dead

1 PLAYS WITHIN PLAYS: STOPPARD ON *Hamlet* AND *Waiting for Godot*

Rosencrantz and Guildenstern Are Dead burst upon the London stage in its first professional production by the National Theatre at the Old Vic in 1967. In spite of its great popularity – it is probably Tom Stoppard's best known and most often revived stage play – critics have consistently failed to agree about the nature of Stoppard's artistic achievement. In trying to understand how exactly *Rosencrantz and Guildenstern Are Dead* succeeds as a piece of theatre one might begin by attempting to account for the play's popularity.

The play is not, I suggest, a serious literary-critical commentary on Shakespeare's *Hamlet*. The insights Stoppard has to offer on that play are not of the kind which derive from an expert close reading of Shakespeare's text. Stoppard starts by assuming the status of *Hamlet* as mythic Shakespearean drama – as *the* play which represents the image of Shakespearean tragedy to the vast majority of non-scholars who yet maintain a vague notion about English drama. Whether or not one has read *Hamlet* – and the vast majority of people probably know something about the play without ever having read it – Shakespeare's tragedy has an archetypal significance, evoking a theatrical style of rhetorical bombast which in turn suggests vivid if generalised notions about the dilemma of a sensitive individual confronted by a corrupt society.

Some will have an image of *Hamlet* as an ineffectual procrastinator, a brooding over-sensitive soul who fails to act when confronted by the harsh realities of power politics. Others may associate the name with a noble and righteous

prince, quick to assume his predestined role as avenger of
his father's death but nevertheless, because of his tragic
failure to act as ruthlessly as his opponents, ironically
responsible for the virtual massacre of the dramatis personae
at the end of the play. Most people who speak English have
heard the phrase 'To be or not to be' which begins Hamlet's
most famous soliloquy in Act III. These facts or opinions
about the play are widely known.

But only a small minority of people who know something
of the play are conversant with the precise details of its
structure and significance. Stoppard's strategy is to exploit
the gaps between the folklore status of *Hamlet* as archetypal
'Shakespeare-tragedy' and the orthodox academic interpretations of *Hamlet* as an intricately wrought and subtly articulated text which expresses a complex set of reflections on
human actions and motives. *Rosencrantz and Guildenstern Are
Dead* flatters an uneducated audience into thinking that they
know *Hamlet* better than they do by building up a seemingly
coherent image of the *Hamlet*-world which Stoppard is simultaneously in the process of deconstructing. (You do not
actually need to know *Hamlet* to enjoy *Rosencrantz and Guildenstern Are Dead* in the theatre.)

For the advanced Shakespeare student or critic, Stoppard
does not offer a serious interrogation of Shakespeare's text.
What the play does – with coruscating wit – is to offer a
sophisticated pastiche of the clichés of Shakespeare interpretation as the basis upon which Stoppard elaborates his reflections on contemporary experience. But Stoppard does this
apparently within the confines of Shakespeare's *Hamlet*-
world. For it is Rosencrantz and Guildenstern, themselves
characters existing within the world of Shakespeare's
tragedy, who provide the parodic critical perspective on that
world.

One reason why the play has been so consistently popular
has been its direct appeal to the undergraduate student in
each of us. It permits us to genuflect to the myth of Shakespeare – 'not for an age but for all time' – at the same time as
it makes philistine jokes about how irrelevant Shakespearean
tragedy is to the actualities of the present, and how preten-
tious and bombastic Shakespeare's language sounds when

applied to situations which call to mind the banal trivialities of our everyday life.

While also consciously exploiting a number of the well-known theatrical motifs in Beckett's *Waiting for Godot*, Stoppard's play is not merely an attempt to rewrite *Godot* within the framework of Shakespeare's drama. More pointedly, it is an arch and rueful attempt to question the possible significance of Shakespearean tragedy for a young adult in the second half of the twentieth century. The source of the play's humour, as with much of Stoppard's comedy, lies in the deliberate mismatching of Elizabethan form with contemporary experience, and from the yoking together of a late twentieth-century idiom with Elizabethan political actions and social values. *Rosencrantz and Guildenstern Are Dead* is a camp and complicated version of an undergraduate joke, self-consciously jostling the elitist assumptions of the high culture against the philistine habits of the low.

In Shakespeare's play, Rosencrantz and Guildenstern are little more than functionaries. Fellow-students of the Prince at the University of Wittenberg, they have been summoned to Elsinore by Hamlet's uncle Claudius and his mother Gertrude, who had married Claudius shortly after the death of her late husband King Hamlet. The first indications in the text are that they have been brought to the court of Denmark to cheer up their friend the Prince. But by Act III, Scene 1 it might appear that Claudius is using them to spy on Hamlet whom he vaguely suspects of intending some malice towards him.

In Act IV Claudius and Gertrude treat Rosencrantz and Guildenstern as henchmen, entrusting the supposedly mad and potentially dangerous Hamlet to their care after his stabbing of Polonius, whom he had mistaken for Claudius. They appear in *Hamlet* for the last time in Act IV, Scene 3 after which their death at the hands of the King of England is reported in Act V. So although they play a large part in shaping the outcome of the second half of Shakespeare's plot, they are relatively unimportant characters in terms of their involvement in events actually presented on the stage.

It was in the late Victorian period that Rosencrantz and Guildenstern first achieved a literary-theatrical prominence which Shakespeare's play had denied them. In the well-established Victorian tradition of Shakespearean travesty, W. S. Gilbert had in 1891 written a burlesque version of *Hamlet* called *Rosencrantz and Guildenstern*. Gilbert did not offer any serious insights into either the play or the role of Hamlet's student companions. His intention was merely to parody the formal conventions of Elizabethan tragedy, milking Shakespeare's rhetoric for as many cheap laughs as possible.

In a paragraph of *De Profundis* (1896) Oscar Wilde had offered the first serious reflection on the significance of the two characters:

> I know nothing in all drama more incomparable from the point of view of art, nothing more suggestive in its subtlety of observation, than Shakespeare's drawing of Rosencrantz and Guildenstern. . . . At the moment when they come across him [Hamlet] . . . he is staggering under the weight of a burden intolerable to one of his temperament. The dead have come armed out of the grave to impose on him a mission at once too great and too mean for him. He is a dreamer, and he is called upon to act. He has the nature of the poet, and he is asked to grapple with the common complexity of cause and effect, with life and its practical realisation, of which he knows nothing, not within life in its ideal essence, of which he knows so much. He has no conception of what to do, and his folly is to feign folly. . . . Instead of trying to be the hero of his own history, he seeks to be the spectator of his own tragedy. He disbelieves in everything, including himself. . . . Of all this Guildenstern and Rosencrantz realise nothing. They bow and smirk and smile, and what one says the other echoes with sickliest intonation. . . . They are close to . . . [Hamlet's] very secret and know nothing of it. Nor would there be any use in telling them. They are the little cups that can hold so much and no more. Towards the close it is suggested that, caught in a cunning springe set for another, they have met, or may meet, with a violent and sudden death. But a tragic ending of this kind . . . is really not for such as they. They never die . . . They are types fixed for all time . . . They are merely out of their sphere.
>
> (*De Profundis, Works of Oscar Wilde* (1966 edn), pp. 949–50)

T. S. Eliot's *The Love Song of J. Alfred Prufrock* (1917)

extended Wilde's notion of the insignificance of Hamlet's college friends to emphasise the poignancy of the contrast between two innocents wondering aimlessly through the political intrigues of Shakespeare's Denmark, and Hamlet himself, fully aware of the complex demands of his situation, yet unable until the end of Act V to perform the heroic action which is his destiny. In the words of Eliot's anxious modern anti-hero, J. Alfred Prufrock:

> No! I am not Prince Hamlet, nor was meant to be;
> Am an attendant lord, one that will do
> To swell a progress, start a scene or two,
> Advise the prince; no doubt, an easy tool,
> Deferential, glad to be of use,
> Politic, cautious, and meticulous;
>
>   (ll. 112–17)

The figure of the hero as passive sufferer or witness began in the early part of the twentieth century to replace the traditionally active hero of earlier tragedy. The poetry and drama of T. S. Eliot and the work of the major figures associated with the modernist movement such as Joyce, Faulkner, Virginia Woolf, Kafka and Samuel Beckett, centre upon the subjective consciousness of a central character who suffers or witnesses the great events of life rather than actively initiating or shaping them. Many of the most vividly realised characters of the new wave of plays in the late 1950s and early 1960s were comically or flamboyantly anti-heroic. The most famous of these were Vladimir and Estragon in Beckett's *Waiting for Godot*, Jimmy Porter in Osborne's *Look Back in Anger* and Stanley in Pinter's *The Birthday Party*. All three of these writers are much admired by Stoppard.

Vladimir and Estragon in *Waiting for Godot* are lost in a wasteland whose only distinguishing features are a country road and a tree. A critic once commented that in *Godot*, 'Nothing happens, twice', an aptly witty comment on the way in which the second act mimics the apparent randomness of the plot in Act I. In fact the action of *Godot* presents the experience of two tramp-like figures (Vladimir and Estragon) who repeatedly attempt to leave the place by the tree where they are waiting to meet a certain Mr Godot. Up to this moment in their lives Godot has never arrived. But towards evening every day, a boy appears with a cryptic message that suggests Mr Godot will come the following day.

To pass the time until Godot arrives, Vladimir and Estragon go through a series of banal routines such as eating carrots, taking off and putting on shoes, arguing about where they are and where each one slept the previous evening. The most vivid event in each act is the entrance of two men called Pozzo and Lucky, an odd master-and-servant pair who are attached to each other by a rope and who constitute a rather sado-masochistic spectacle somewhat voyeuristically enjoyed by Vladimir and Estragon as a relief from their own rather more mundane bouts of bickering and reconciliation.

Waiting for Godot challenges the assumption that any general significance can be given to human existence. To conduct his interrogation of everyday habits of thinking and belief in theatrical form, Beckett plays with an audience's basic expectations of drama, presenting us with a two-act play without narrative. Constituted from the structures of the lived experience of space, time and human identity, apparently without the imposition of literary conventions such as narrative or psychological conventions of character, *Waiting for Godot* denies an audience any sociological or psychological framework for interpreting the behaviour of the dramatis personae.

A casual comparison of *Rosencrantz and Guildenstern Are Dead* with *Waiting for Godot* will reveal how profoundly Beckett has influenced Stoppard's view of the theatre and of life. In an interview, Stoppard himself has described how he feels the influence of *Waiting for Godot:*

> There's just no telling what sort of effect it had on our society, who wrote because of it, or wrote in a different way because of it. But it really redefined the minima of theatrical experience. . . . Of course it would be absurd to deny my enormous debt to it. To me the representative attitude is 'I am a human being . . .' Beckett gives me more pleasure than I can express because he always ends up with a man surrounded by the wreckage of a proposition he had made in confidence only two minutes before.
>
> ('Something to Declare', *Sunday Times*, 25 February 1968)

But a comparison between *Godot* and *Rosencrantz and Guildenstern Are Dead* will also reveal distinct differences between Stoppard's play and that of Beckett. While it is obvious that Stoppard has derived elements of the situation of two apparently – though not actually – interchangeable and interdependent characters who are somehow condemned by life to wait while they observe and interrogate the monotony of an unchanging situation in which a few actual events recur with very slight variations to the point of tedium, the locations of the plays differ significantly. It would seem unthinkable for Beckett to set a play of his within the subtextual penumbra of another play. While the two writers share a facility with language, a fascination with the histrionic facility which allows people obsessively to dramatise experience, and a tendency to blur the distinction between subjective and objective perspective in the theatre, all of Beckett's plays, even the most minimal or abstract, are located in a concrete and sensuously imagined theatrical space, albeit a space which may be devastatingly barren or so isolated and monochromatic as to evoke a mental landscape.

Stoppard, on the other hand, while seeming to establish a more ordinary location for his plays, makes use of such easily recognisable conventions of setting that their very theatricality becomes the image of the fictional world the plays create. *Rosencrantz and Guildenstern Are Dead* established what has since become virtually a working principle of Stoppard's theatrical writing. The setting of each play is specifically designed to draw attention to its own artifice. By so doing, it requires the audience consciously to conceive the medium of each work as a prism through which to view a world which is quite obviously an artificial construct but which constitutes a model useful for demonstrating certain truths about the complexities of human experience. The important thing to remember is that no action presented on stage need be perceived as a direct representation of an aspect of experience. The performance is a game played in such a way as to focus certain features of experience as problems to be confronted and rationalised. Even when Stoppard comes closest to writing in a naturalistic mode, as in his television play *Professional Foul*, he consciously exploits a self-referentiality which is made possible by the medium of television just as much as it is by the theatre. That is surely the reason for his introduction of the parallel story of the journalists reporting on an international football match taking place in Prague at the same time as the Colloquium on Moral Philosophy. The presence of journalists reporting on a football match motivates the naturalistic presentation of all the action according to the conventions of tele-documentary, ensuring not merely that we will respond to the Hollar family's authentic experience of political oppression as fact, but also allowing us to respond to the thematic connections of 'playing the game' which relate the footballers, the moral philosophers and the oppressed population of Prague with the kind of concern usually evoked by the factuality of a TV documentary.

With hindsight *Rosencrantz and Guildenstern Are Dead* can be seen as Stoppard's attempt to announce and perfect the terms of his art, to establish the rules of the game he intends to play with theatre. By using a device which Marowitz called 'a play-beneath-the-play-*Hamlet*', Stoppard motivates his own baroque recreation of contemporary drama. He is able elegantly and without straining to set the *Hamlet* world in the wings of the *Godot* world and vice versa because his own aesthetic is *neither* that of Shakespeare *nor* that of Beckett. Stoppard is perhaps best characterised as a post-modernist writer, someone who self-consciously interrogates and reflects upon the fragments of the culture he has inherited. He does not build his plays out of direct experience, although they may often evoke actual experience in the minds of spectators; he builds them from the skeletons of older plays and older forms of entertainment.

So inevitably, in order to express his own view of life Stoppard must first question, parody, deconstruct, ridicule and occasionally celebrate the values inherent in the traditional cultural forms which constitute the base structure of his own work. His own view of life can only be expressed ironically – in terms of a tension between the farcical deconstruction of the old forms in the process of which new meanings are discovered and new attitudes to life experienced. All of the really urgent moments in Stoppard's theatre derive their poignancy or comic impact from the disintegration which ironically and unexpectedly detaches these moments from the surrounding theatrical artifice. Because of the necessity to distinguish the felt intensity of authentic revelation from the parodic presentation of a range of intellectual systems, some of the most significant moments in the plays are often missed if they are not seen in performance.

2   WHEELS WITHIN WHEELS: THE PLOT AS FATE

One of the most remarkable aspects of Stoppard's achievement in *Rosencrantz and Guildenstern Are Dead* is his creation of a completely new work from Shakespeare's *Hamlet*. Apart from the actual quotations from Act II, Scene 1, Act II, Scene 2, Act II, Scenes 1, 2, and 3, Act IV, Scenes 1 and 2, and Act V, Scene 1 of Shakespeare's play the stage action is Stoppard's invention. Less than one-tenth of the text consists of quotations from *Hamlet*, yet Stoppard manages to write a new play without altering Shakespeare's underlying plot structure at all. He merely presents it from the point of view of two minor characters in a manner which appears to improvise action for Rosencrantz and Guildenstern in the gaps which Shakespeare has left with respect to incidents which might have bearing on the central events even if they are merely tributary to it.

By doing this he ensures that a contemporary audience shares the dilemma of Rosencrantz and Guildenstern, creating an image of ordinary people confronted by an order of existence which they do not fully perceive and over which they have no control. The irony of the play consists in the fact that the audience witnesses Rosencrantz and Guildenstern improvising their lives in a Beckettian fashion to form a pre-existing pattern which that audience already knows. Rosencrantz and Guildenstern seem forced to choose how to respond to every demand made and every possibility offered by an existential situation which, while we recognise it as the plot of *Hamlet*, is to the characters the authentic social and political arena about whose periphery their lives revolve.

Perhaps the central point which Stoppard's play makes is that Rosencrantz and Guildenstern do not *choose* any genuine course of action, they merely improvise stage business to pass away the time, questioning the action of *Hamlet* and their problematic location within it in a way which provides a running critical commentary on that play. They die, or in theatrical terms merely disappear, as they do because in one sense they have failed to do more than improvise dialogue and stage business when the plot of *Hamlet* actually implies the possibility that by refusing to execute Claudius' scheme they might save Hamlet and themselves. Stoppard is, in this respect, more critical of his two main characters than is Beckett in *Waiting for Godot*.

Stoppard's plot inventions are as follows:

1. The meeting of Rosencrantz and Guildenstern with the players in Act I.
2. Their conversation with the Player and the rehearsal of *The Mousetrap* around which Stoppard places actual snippets of scenes from Acts II, III and IV of *Hamlet* and invents reactions for Rosencrantz and Guildenstern not supplied by Shakespeare, but which form a pattern of plausible response to and motivation for the actual intrigue which culminates in Hamlet's slaughter of Polonius in *Hamlet*, Act III, Scene 3.
3. The action on board a ship bound for England. This is entirely Stoppard's invention although it does not in any way alter the narrative structure of *Hamlet*; rather it extends the offstage events which are reported in Act V, Scene I of *Hamlet*, representing them as onstage action.

The plot of *Hamlet* therefore becomes a metaphor for human destiny in Stoppard's play: Rosencrantz and Guildenstern succumb to a destiny which is predetermined for them by Shakespeare. Stoppard, however, emphasises the possibility that Rosencrantz and Guildenstern could change their fate (i.e. alter the plot of *Hamlet*) by choosing *not* to be so passive in obeying Claudius' instructions: the audience is continually made aware in *Rosencrantz and Guildenstern Are Dead* of moments of choice in which the protagonists, by surrendering to the movement of events around them rather than determining events themselves, fail to assert their free will. What is comic from Stoppard's perspective is the way in which they *allow* themselves to become pawns in the political chess game between Hamlet and Claudius, just as they automatically assume the role of spectators to the Players.

Rosencrantz and Guildenstern Are Dead ironically reveals the protagonists' potential freedom to be actors rather than spectators. The possibility that they could either choose to be conscious deceivers (like the Player) or genuinely political (like Hamlet) implies their ability either to transform their minor roles in a prescripted drama into central roles in the authentic conflicts of moral and political life, or at the least to escape a pointless death. The title of the play, reminding an audience that these two minor characters in Shakespeare have become major characters in another play, establishes its central irony. Yet equally Stoppard's play makes it perfectly understandable that they fail to act. The music hall style of the improvised games and patter (derived directly from *Godot*) which Rosencrantz and Guildenstern employ to pass the time comically emphasises the distance between the average person's moment-to-moment obsession with trivia and the central arena of political reality which circumscribes one's freedom and creates a framework in which those trivia attain a significance, whether or not actually intended by the individual.

Using the conventions of the *Godot* world the play confronts us with an image of everyday existence as theatrical tedium. From this perspective it seems that it would make no difference what the two hapless protagonists did. The *Hamlet* world appears as an absurdly stereotyped melodrama, a game whose rules are rigidly established and in which Rosencrantz and Guildenstern can only make the moves which have been predetermined for them. All of life seems like an old play in which Rosencrantz and Guildenstern's only freedom lies in playing silly games like tossing a coin or improvising word-play and philosophical speculation in an attempt to find out what rules govern the behaviour of the powerful individuals they only glimpse in passing. In theatrical terms theirs is an attempt to discover what conventions govern a performance of the play *Hamlet*.

As in real life, the rules are not manifest until the individuals are dead. Life can be seen to be a game whose moves are not rationally coherent while it is being experienced: the underlying pattern becomes manifest only at the moment of death. An awareness of this fact causes so much anxiety to the protagonists that they spend their time actually indulging in conscious game-playing because they cannot believe that time might have authentic meaning as experience.

If, as Rosencrantz suggests, there are wheels within wheels, it is because Stoppard's creation of a completely new play within the framework of a well-known old play reveals this to be both a cliché and a profound revelation about the human condition. One could say that because they insist on behaving like characters in a Beckett play, Rosencrantz and Guildenstern end up suffering the casual death of minor characters in a Shakespearean tragedy. It is precisely because they fail to intervene decisively in the action of *Hamlet* – to act heroically in terms of the conventions of Elizabethan tragedy – that they end up dead. This is made clear at the outset by means of the play's title. In this sense then, the protagonists achieve a destiny wholly different from any character in a Beckett play. If Beckett's characters are discovered at the beginning of a play in the middle of a slow process of dying, they are never actually dead at the end of the play, only a little further advanced in their decrepitude.

Although much influenced by *Waiting for Godot, Rosencrantz and Guildenstern Are Dead* is certainly not unknowingly derivative. It self-consciously exploits the gulf between Beckett's world and Shakespeare's, asserting the contemporary relevance of both writers as a dialectical tension between the world view of each.

3   GEORGE VS THE LOGICAL POSITIVISTS: STOPPARD ON PHILOSOPHY

> When I first asked . . . [Stoppard] what the play was about, . . . [he] said, 'It's about a man trying to write a lecture'. But for me it was about a man trying to write a lecture *while his wife was stuck with a corpse in the next room.*
> (Programme note, National Theatre revival of *Jumpers*, 1976)

In thus describing the action of *Jumpers*, Peter Wood, the director of the first production of the play for the National Theatre, put his finger on the device which so brilliantly motivates the play's dialectic of intellectual argument and theatrical entertainment. The play in fact interweaves and interrelates Dotty's human dilemma with George's intellectual problems in order to provoke reflection on the human implications of a widely held philosophical viewpoint. In itself, Stoppard's idea of dramatising the process of writing a lecture is brilliantly original. Readers of the play may be so fascinated by the picture of an academic philosopher at work that they may on first encountering *Jumpers* be misled into assuming that Stoppard aims merely to illustrate the point of George Moore's lecture. Following the progress of his argument will involve an enormous degree of concentration on the part of a reader and the intellectual debate might appear to be the major focus of the play.

On the other hand, audiences seeing the play in the theatre are more likely to respond to the comic business and to interpret George's refusal to face his wife's emotional state and to deal with the breakdown of his marriage as an irony which in existential terms reveals the comedy of George's hapless attempt to prove the existence of God through the proper application of philosophical logic. (If he cannot see the reality of his wife's nervous breakdown under his own nose, how can he possibly hope to resolve the central problems which have baffled philosophers for thousands of years?) A full response to the play in the theatre requires an audience to comprehend the relationship between both aspects of the drama – the intellectual argument and the existential situation within which the argument is located. It must be said that to follow the import of George's argument in detail may seem to require a competence in the methods of academic philosophy which the average theatre-goer does not possess. Because of this, productions of the play run the risk of undermining the seriousness of George's struggle to establish by means of rational argument a convincing proof for the existence of God as a preliminary step towards determining a proper basis for morality. By assuming that the audience will not be able to grasp the detail of the argument, and thus playing up the image of George as a stereotypical absent-minded professor, actors may be tempted to burlesque the lecture, reducing it to a jumble of academic philosopher's jargon delivered to the audience in the manner of Lucky's chaotic stream-of-consciousness monologue in *Waiting for Godot*.

But this is surely not the playwright's intention. One of Stoppard's finest qualities as an entertainer is that he makes unexpected demands of an audience. It is part of the comic shock effect of a Stoppard play that it requires an audience to yoke together what seem at first to be unrelated ideas or unconnected images. In *Jumpers* we are asked to listen attentively to a complicated lecture on moral philosophy around which is unfolding an incredible whodunnit. As the action of the whodunnit becomes more and more improbable so paradoxically it seems more and more precisely to reflect the disintegrating universe surrounding George Moore and his wife Dotty. In addition it is apparent that this disintegrating universe is a consequence of the pragmatism endemic in public life, an attitude promoted by the triumph of the relativistic philosophy which George's argument is designed to combat.

Once one understands something of the context of twentieth-century philosophical debate to which George's lecture refers, its point is not difficult to grasp. The lecture begins at the traditional starting point of Western philosophy – the branch of metaphysics which aims to account for the origin of the universe. As George himself points out, the attempt

to prove the existence of God is not a purely technical
exercise:

> Because it is to account for two quite unconnected mysteries
> that the human mind looks beyond humanity and it is two
> of him that philosophy obligingly provides. There is, first, the
> God of Creation to account for existence, and, second, the
> God of Goodness to account for moral values. (p. 17)

The proof of the existence of God is necessary to provide
an explanation of how the world as we know it could have
come into existence and also to validate the ethical system
according to which people live. But George's academically
trained mind cannot desist from pursuing the implication
that metaphysics and ethics are not logically connected:

> I say they are unconnected because there is no logical reason
> why the fountainhead of goodness in the universe should have
> necessarily created the universe in the first place, nor is it
> necessary on the other hand, that a Creator should care tup-
> pence about the behaviour of his creations. . . . In practice,
> people admit a Creator to give authority to moral values, and
> admit moral values to give point to the Creation. (p. 17)

The above lines occur only three minutes or so into the
lecture but already George appears in danger of being
hijacked by the circularity which seems inherent in his own
argument. George's rigorous philosophical honesty makes it
virtually impossible to construct a valid argument. The more
open he is in admitting the problems – and Stoppard gets
a good deal of comic mileage out of this – the more his
endeavour appears doomed to failure.

And yet as the play and the lecture progress, the audience
begins to feel more strongly the need for such a proof to
establish the existence of God as a foundation for morality,
especially as the world around George and Dotty threatens
to drift towards a chaos apparently precipitated by the
absence of a coherent moral system. While the action of the
play illustrates with ever increasing urgency the need for
such a demonstration, George's efforts to supply one com-

ically demonstrate the virtual impossibility of constructing
it according to the correct procedures of philosophy.

Set against both Dotty's crisis of belief in the romantic
ideal of true love, symbolised by her inability to remember
the words of her moon songs, and George's faltering attempts
to prove the existence of God as a necessary precondition
for the elaboration of a transcendental value system, is the
concrete demonstration in the play of Archie's pragmatic
triumph as a politician; Archie's ruthless efficiency appears
to be a consequence of his espousal of a wholly relativistic
philosophy that rejects questions of intrinsic value in favour
of a rationalistic and materialistic approach to life. ('No
problem is insoluble given a large enough plastic bag.') The
name given to Archie's acrobatic troupe – and indeed his
own surname – comically emblematises the chief characteristic of this philosophical approach. The jumpers are academics who, just as they spend their professional lives performing feats of mental gymnastics, devote their spare time to
real gymnastics as members of Archie's university team.
Stoppard deliberately draws a comic analogy between the
activities of philosophy and gymnastics in order to illustrate
the relativistic view of morality which is predominant in
contemporary life.

It is implied that the 'new pragmatism in public life' as
evidenced in the election victory ('Archie says it was a coup
d'état') and in the ruthless self-interest evinced by the astronaut Scott, who after a successful moon landing sacrifices
his fellow astronaut's life in order to save his own, are
logical consequences of the acceptance of the rationalistic
philosophy which George so haplessly opposes. The Rad-Lib
philosophy asserts that since the existence of transcendental
values cannot be scientifically proved, such values cannot
be held to exist. Problems of morality and aesthetics are
merely technical problems and philosophy must become
merely a demonstration of intellectual skills analogous to the
exhibition of physical skills in gymnastics. From Archie's
Rad-Lib perspective the focus of philosophy becomes the
study of the linguistic conventions according to which people
categorise and describe their feelings about the world. Moral
and aesthetic values as such are fictions. Every society estab-

lishes its own arbitrary conventions of behaviour, and actions are labelled good or bad merely according to how closely or not they adhere to particular social conventions. Actions cannot be inherently good or bad. Morality becomes a matter of learning the rules of the game and sticking to them, and moral philosophy a glorified technology: the philosopher is reduced to the role of referee or umpire whose function is merely to interpret the rules of the game.

In *Jumpers* Stoppard expresses the opposition between absolute and relativistic views of ethics that we have already seen to underlie the action of *Rosencrantz and Guildenstern Are Dead* and which most of his plays reflect. In doing so, *Jumpers* makes reference to a wide-ranging debate which has been continued in various forms since Logical Positivism was first adumbrated in the 1920s. Without some understanding of the reason why the debate is important, a reader or spectator may not grasp the full seriousness of this sophisticated comedy.

In an interview given two years after the play's first performance, Stoppard explained his own view of the play's central concern. After remarking on the irony that so many rational humanists who are highly sceptical about the kind of mystical attitudes reflected in the theological tradition also read their horoscopes, he suggested that:

> the very fact that horoscopes exist *at all* in a world which is said to be – at least in Western Europe – over sixty per cent non-churchgoing at best, suggests that everybody has a repository of a 'mystical' awareness that there is a lot more to them than meets the microscope. It's a difficult thing to express in terms which are not, if you like, 'spiritual' or 'mystical', but I think that almost everybody would admit to having this sense that some things actually are better than others in a way which is not, in fact, rational.
> (Interview, *Under Bow Bells* (London, 1974), pp. 163–4)

The argument George develops in his lecture largely reflects the point of view which was most famously articulated around the turn of the century by the intuitionist philosopher G. E. Moore in a book called *Principia Ethica*. The fact that the Professor of Moral Philosophy in *Jumpers* is also called George Moore is an irony not lost on the rueful comic hero who seems in his professional life destined to be not merely second-rate but inevitably second. G. E. Moore used logic to try and prove the existence of the world which the faculty of commonsense apprehends as real – not as easy a task as it might sound to a lay person. In order logically to *prove* the existence of the world and consequently of a system of ethical absolutes which a lay person might *intuitively know* to exist, the philosopher must argue backwards from commonsense perceptions to infer the existence of a first cause or God. This Creator establishes the necessary conditions for the existence of the Universe and of a human value system. Without a proof for the existence of such a Creator it is impossible to know whether the evidence of our commonsense perception is real or merely the product of the individual's own subjective consciousness. To satisfy the logical requirements of philosophy this proof must be both the most complete and the most economical explanation of the facts apprehended through commonsense. Significantly, G. E. Moore's work antedates that of the Logical Positivists although his formulation of the problems posed by his own intuitionist approach paradoxically contributed to the development of Logical Positivism as an alternative. This is why George claims that he wants to set philosophy back forty years!

In an interview with Mel Gussow in the *New York Times* on 23 April 1974, Stoppard humorously indicated the importance of George's endeavour from the standpoint of an average man or woman:

> Most of the propositions I'm interested in have been kidnapped and dressed up by academic philosophy, but they are in fact the kind of propositions that would occur to any intelligent person in his bath. They're not academic questions, simply questions which have been given academic status. Philosophy can be reduced to a small number of questions which are battled about in most bars most nights. . . . I've always thought that the idea of God is absolutely preposterous, but slightly more plausible than the alternative position that, given enough time, some green slime could write Shakespeare's sonnets.

George's paper is to be presented at the university symposium as a refutation of a paper intended to be delivered by Duncan McFee, the Professor of Logic in the university. The opposition of Logic (McFee) and Ethics (George), two of the chief branches of traditional philosophy, is deliberate. It is George's commonsense view of ethics which is made to seem illogical and outdated in terms of the position of mainstream contemporary philosophy, while the materialist and relativist viewpoint of McFee and Archie seems logical and effective. We learn from George himself that McFee in his lecture represents (as does Archie in action) the dominant trend in mid-twentieth-century philosophy. As George tells Inspector Bones, who is a detective sent to investigate the murder of a gymnast later discovered to be Duncan McFee himself:

> [McFee] thinks good and bad aren't actually *good* and *bad* in any absolute or metaphysical sense, he believes them to be categories of our making, social and psychological conventions which we have evolved in order to make living in groups a practical possibility in much the same way as we have evolved the rules of tennis without which Wimbledon Fortnight would be a shambles, do you see? (p. 38)

Bones' response to George's explanation that McFee would, for example, regard telling lies and murder as not sinful (inherently bad) but merely anti-social is to ask in a tone of shocked moralism, 'What sort of philosophy is that?' to which an unperturbed George replies, 'Mainstream, I'd call it. Orthodox mainstream!' (p. 39)

On stage the exchange is very funny as it not only rebounds against the clichéd moralism which is a stock-in-trade of the stereotypical stage detective but also reveals George's total absorption in the arguments of academic philosophy which appear wholly at odds with the audience's commonsense perception of morality. Ironically, George is merely outlining the mainstream philosophical standpoint which he is at such pains throughout the play to refute. This Rad-Lib philosophy is Stoppard's fictionalised version of Logical Positivism, one of the most influential movements in twentieth-century philosophy.

The principles of Logical Positivism were adumbrated in the 1920s by a group of scientists and philosophers at the University of Vienna known as the 'Vienna Circle'. Their idea was that philosophy did not exist as an independent discipline. The only meaningful statements were scientific propositions: a statement could only be said to be true or false if it could actually or possibly be verified according to the methods of the physical sciences. Some of the traditional branches of philosophy, specifically Metaphysics, Ethics and Aesthetics, were no longer regarded as valid subjects for philosophical investigation as they were not susceptible of scientific verification. Statements about metaphysics, morality and art were merely expressions of feeling, whereas statements of fact were subject to strict scientific proof. If philosophers wished to maintain an interest in such subjects they would have to confine themselves to analysing the conventions and usage of language which govern the expression of feelings about morality or art. Human values as such could no longer be regarded as having any meaning other than that determined by social conventions which operate like the rules of a game or as psychological norms which regulate human behaviour in accordance with the principles of neurology.

It is in the interests of a more humane philosophy that George Moore pits himself against such a modern Establishment.

4   LITERARY-DRAMATIC PASTICHE: THE PLOT AS A GAME

If the unifying intellectual theme of *Jumpers* resides in George's attempt to prove that it is more rational to accept the mystery of God than to surrender to the wholly relativistic standpoint of Logical Positivism, then the play's theatrical structure develops and illustrates this idea in the fullest possible way. The idea is comically formulated in the most general terms when George cries in mock anguish three-quarters of the way through the play, 'How the hell does one know what to believe?' (p. 62). At this moment George's suspicions as to whether or not Archie is having an affair with Dotty are at their height, so his question may be taken to refer to Dotty and Archie; but it also occurs at a point when George is beginning to despair of satisfactorily clinching the argument of his paper, and the line is a clever reduction to a colloquial level of the question which George has been repeatedly reformulating in technical terms throughout the play. Plainly speaking, this is the most general statement of the overall theme of *Jumpers*: nothing in the world is what it seems to be. Appearances cannot ever be congruent with reality. The most bizarre and unconvincing explanations of the theatrical events being performed seem to be the only philosophically acceptable ones. Explanations of the ever-increasing confusion which constitutes the play's action are offered but they seem so incredible ('Credibility is an expanding field') that the play leaves open the possibility that the audience may decide not to believe them.

Stoppard's great achievement is to provide us with theatrical images of the inexplicable absurdity of the world we inhabit and at the same time to offer a series of logically coherent explanations which would account for all the facts given in the course of the action. Although we may try solving the mystery of the whodunnit if we so choose, such a resolution of the plot does not clinch the central philosophical argument, neither does it resolve the existential dilemma faced by George and Dotty. Having brought us to a point of recognition of the need for some kind of absolute value system, Stoppard shows us through the character of Archie the triumph of rationalistic philosophy and, in consequence, the world in a process of gradual auto-destruction. *Jumpers* works as brilliantly as it does because the play creates a theatrical world which in its own eccentric way is yet recognisable as a comic reflection of our everyday domestic existence. While offering a jokey but nevertheless consistent explanation of the surreal cocktail of strange coincidences and bizarre incidents which constitutes the play's action, the sophisticated artfulness which characterises the complicated

plot signifies that truth, besides being more complex than fiction, is inevitably stranger.

The tension of the plot does not reside in the building up of suspense about the danger which the characters are in (as in a certain type of thriller), nor is the plot seriously constructed around the classic detective whodunnit formula in which the crime has been committed before the play starts and in which the action consists of the successive discovery of pieces of incriminating evidence against each character until the identity of the culprit becomes obvious. However, both these motifs are jokingly alluded to: Bones *does* actually arrive in the time-honoured manner of the plodding local police inspector to investigate a crime which has taken place at George and Dotty's flat, and in the coda, Archbishop Clegthorpe *is* actually shot, a surprise reversal of the who-dunnit conventions which at the end of the play ironically suggests that it may have been more to the point if the audience *had* regarded the play as a genuine whodunnit, rather than a philosophical argument.

Through the use of his characteristic collage technique of setting one stock literary or theatrical form against another, Stoppard teases an audience with regard to what response would be appropriate to the human situation embodied in the play. If the question subliminally present throughout the play is 'How the hell do I know what to believe?', Stoppard's complex interweaving of the alternative perspectives provided by the dazzling array of literary and theatrical forms articulates a question reiterated in each of his plays: What framework of interpretation is relevant in the attempt to comprehend the complex and usually conflicting perspectives which form the core structures of human experience?

Each theatrical incident means something different when viewed through a different prism. Dotty's experience of find-ing herself literally with a dead jumper on her hands is transformed according to the particular perspective in which it is viewed. Presumably each member of the audience will perceive each incident in the play in terms of the particular frame of reference that individual brings to the theatrical experience. Stoppard contrives the action of the play to create a montage of alternative perspectives on the play's basic situation. In a realist work of art there is an underlying assumption that a single unifying interpretation of the work is possible, based on the integration of all the separately perceived aspects and elements which constitute the reader's or spectator's experience of the work. While the artist may evoke the complexity of felt experience through presentation of a tapestry woven from the minutiae of day-to-day experiences, the overall design of a realist work reveals the coherence of a single point of view or subjective consciousness – that of the artist.

The aim of a work like *Jumpers* is to interrogate and perhaps finally to destroy the spectator's presuppositions concerning the overall coherence of a dramatic work, not by offering a wholly anarchic piece of theatrical nonsense (as in a Dada performance) but by offering instead a subtle dramatic illustration of the way reality begins to seem ever more complex and unknowable the more rigorously it is subjected to rational analysis. To this end, the opening fifteen minutes of *Jumpers* consist of a bravura theatrical collage (like a Dada performance or a Futurist event) which makes reference now to one set of audience expectations, now to another, deliberately and repeatedly disorienting the audience as it is invited to construe the significance of colliding images which dissolve one into the other, reminding a spectator of the kaleidoscopic effect of film or television montage. And yet unlike the typical montage of images in a TV detective thriller (e.g. *The Avengers*), whose sequence normally begins to make sense after twenty or thirty seconds, this theatrical montage cannot be read according to the ordinary conventions of film or television viewing. On the surface, the function of this opening sequence is to entertain the audience with a circus or cabaret of theatrical surprises. Skilfully interwoven through the theatrical images and performance tricks, however, are the major threads of exposition which would usually be unobtrusively inserted into the conversation of the various characters as the first phase of the action in a conventional stage play.

There is a moment in Stoppard's one-act farce *The Real Inspector Hound* (first performance, 17 June 1968) in which the characters start playing a card game which seems to change inexplicably from poker to bridge to snap and ends up as a game of chess! This burlesque of the hackneyed stage business characteristic of the well-made Agatha Christie type of stage whodunnit could almost provide a model for the pattern of the action in *Jumpers*. A number of different theatrical conventions are being applied to the presentation of a central incident (the murder of McFee) and the farce structure deliberately obscures the nature of the theatrical game being played at any particular moment. By the end of the play the audience might feel that such a comic representation of a confusion of codes reflects the dizzying uncertainties of contemporary life. Our experience of the world invites explanation from a bewildering range of perspectives, but the problem then exists of how to integrate these multiple and sometimes contradictory explanations to form a unified view of the situation.

To put it another way, the proliferation of numbers of different scientific and pseudo-scientific disciplines enables us to see the various aspects of the world in more and more complex ways and from more and more varied angles, yet each of these might be said either to negate or else to reduce the significance of the others as each discipline assumes the primacy of its own standpoint and assimilates other views within its own overall perspective. The existence of such a multiplicity of disciplines also renders the classical project of a universal education impossible: the notion is jokingly alluded to in Archie's cynical pretence that his jumpers team represents a version of the ancient Greek ideal of 'mens sana in corpore sana'.

The prologue sequence, which will be analysed in more detail in Part Two of this book, concludes (although in fact Stoppard brilliantly exploits the 'perpetuum mobile' effect of classic farce to ensure that the action never stops) with the image of Dorothy Moore, the hostess of the rather wild party which has just broken up, at one side of the stage holding on to the corpse of a gymnast who seems to have been shot at the climax of an acrobatic display, and her husband George at the other side dictating to his secretary the words, 'To begin at the beginning: Is God?'

The audience's laughter at the incongruity of this por-

tentous philosophical question in the context both of the
preceding mayhem and of George's unknowing exclusion of
his wife's predicament from his own sphere of attention,
involves the first clear sign of the collision between philosophy and show business – the two worlds which for the
remainder of the performance will compete for the audience's
attention. But what kind of show business routine is it that
concludes with a glamorous singing star propping up a
corpse? From this moment, the situation precipitated by
Dotty's party routine will continually interrupt the progress
of George's composition of a paper for the philosophy symposium on 'Man, good, bad or indifferent', until philosophy
and show business merge in the coda, representing George's
nightmare vision of the symposium. However, we might also
view the arc of the play's action as a cabaret or circus
routine interrupted by a series of mishaps which includes
the star's inability to remember the lines of her songs, the
murder of one of the acrobats in the act; and in particular,
by George who persists in introducing irrelevant fragments
of long-winded speculation into the musical routine as he
strays across the stage in the middle of Dorothy's act to
search for his pet hare, Thumper. In the context of Dorothy's
performance, George's appearances are like the accidental
intrusions of a surreptitious stage doorkeeper in a provincial
weekly repertory company's disastrous performance of a
romantic musical comedy. From the standpoint of a Professor of Moral Philosophy earnestly engaged in attempting
to find rational solutions to some of the most vexed questions
about the origin of the universe and the foundation of ethics,
Dotty's hysterical exhibition of neurosis appears as a ludi-
crous intrusion of banal domestic trivialities into a highbrow
world of abstract intellectual argument.

But then why does George's lecture include an experiment
resembling one of Aesop's fables which involves a live tortoise and a hare, a clown-like demonstration using his right
and left socks as examples and an onstage archery display
whose slapstick comic bathos plainly undermines George's
assertion that logically an arrow can never reach its target?
Is he not as much an exhibitionist – an entertainer – as
Dotty? Is his symposium paper merely a desperate attempt

to keep an over-sophisticated theatre audience entertained by philosophical word-games? ('My method of inquiry this evening into certain aspects of this hardy perennial may strike some of you as overly engaging, but experience has taught me that to attempt to sustain the attention of rival schools of academics by argument alone is tantamount to constructing a Gothic arch out of junket.') And why does Dotty's routine about the 'Juney old moon' transform itself at certain points into a poetic and philosophical discourse on the destruction of the romantic absolutes enshrined in love songs and love poems, a destruction occasioned by astronauts' physical exploration of the moon's surface? Two theatrical games are being played simultaneously. A play about a show business routine going awry has been conflated with a play about a Professor of Ethics whose scrupulously rational scrutiny of his own presuppositions persistently undermines his attempts to prove his thesis.

And from the moment when Inspector Bones enters, a third set of theatrical conventions is supplied – that of the stage whodunnit. Yet even this whodunnit (one of the most hackneyed forms of commercial theatre) is not uncontaminated by other literary or theatrical forms. Bones' absurd appearance at the front door, carrying a bouquet of flowers and with one of Dotty's records tucked under his arm, comically undercuts the seriousness of the whodunnit plot now being introduced, by bringing on stage one of the stock characters from a sentimental backstage story – the star's lonely and emotionally unstable fan. Is Bones a type-character in Dotty's saga of the trials-and-tribulations-of-a-neurotic-chanteuse? Or is the whole show business setting merely a colourful background for what is to become an ingenious murder mystery? Here again, a parallel with George's philosophical enquiry suggests itself, for sophisticated detective fiction usually involves logical deduction on a level as abstract as the highest forms of mathematics or logical analysis.

As a result of Bones' police investigation the initial situation of the play is open to various possible explanations, each of which makes reference to a further framework of interpretation.

First, at the head of Bones' list of possible culprits is Dotty. Bones' initial assumptions derive from the stereotypes of show business mythology. In this perspective the mental instability which has prevented glamorous Dorothy Moore from returning to the musical comedy stage caused her to shoot McFee in a moment of emotional confusion. Bones' obsessional belief in such show business clichés would force all the details of the play's action into the time-honoured formula of the star's desperate and unsuccessful attempt to effect a theatrical come-back. The reason why this is funny is that, in spite of its banal, second-hand ring of cliché, the audience's view of the prologue and the play's initial situation might support such an explanation.

Second, if George is the culprit, as he himself inadvertently suggests, then a number of motives for the murder might be plausible, each of which opens up other stereotypical scenarios which would account for the events of the play. In the first place, George may be merely taking the blame for Dotty. This explanation evokes a scenario of the devoted husband and fan who is prepared to sacrifice his own life to save that of his wife (again a melodramatic motif from a backstage saga, but now with a long-standing love affair thrown in). Secondly, George might have done it as an act of revenge against Archie whom he suspects of having an affair with Dotty. (McFee was one of Archie's prized jumpers, as well as having been a major adherent of the tenets of Rad-Lib philosophy.) In this case, sexual jealousy is the prime motive: here the *crime passionel* scenario of a glamorous stage star being fought over by her different lovers is evoked. A clue which points to this interpretation is planted when George makes a joking *Hamlet* allusion ('Now might I do it, Pat') implying that in spite of his ineptitude as a practical politician he might want to murder Archie himself. Thirdly, George could have murdered McFee in order to step into his shoes as Professor of Logic. George does ask Archie minutes after he has learnt of McFee's death, if he could fill the vacant Chair of Logic. This scenario conjures up images of a competitive world of university politics in which George is a Macbeth-figure (again, there are *Macbeth* allusions to substantiate this), ruthlessly determined to succeed in his professional career.

Third, Archie appears to present himself to Inspector Bones as a suspect. A possible motive is supplied by Archie himself. As a result of a crisis of faith, McFee had deserted his position as champion of the Rad-Lib philosophy represented by the jumpers and was going over to support George's belief in moral absolutes, thus undermining the university consensus in favour of Archie's form of moral relativism. In this case, Archie's intention would be to try and make it look as though Dotty did it. Again the Shakespearean allusions reinforce an image of the sinister world of *realpolitik* in which Archie is the Macbeth to George's Banquo. The play has begun with a celebration of the Rad-Lib election victory which Archie claims was a coup d'état, not a general election. And Archie presents himself as a Renaissance man whose political ambitions do not seem to stop at being Vice Chancellor of the university: 'I'm a doctor of medicine, philosophy, literature and law, with diplomas in psychological medicine and P.T. including gym' (p. 52). In the coda, Archie misquotes lines from Shakespeare's *Richard III*: these lines imply a comparison between Archie and Shakespeare's Machiavellian, role-playing villain. Although Bones is not fully aware of this context of interpretation, the whole framework of the play invites the audience to interpret the shooting of McFee as one phase of a large-scale political take-over in which British democracy has been destroyed and in the context of which the particular moral questions with which George is so passionately concerned have been rendered obsolete. But as far as Bones is concerned, Archie may be merely covering up Dotty's guilt. His 'backstage crime saga' interpretation is suddenly undermined by Archie's insistence that 'McFee suffering from nervous strain brought on by the appalling pressure of overwork – for which I blame myself entirely – left here last night in a mood of deep depression and wandered into the park where he crawled into a large, plastic bag and shot himself' (p. 55). This explanation exploits the sentimental stereotype solution of pulp detective fiction with outrageous implausibility. Through his unblushing manipulation of the clichés of the genre, Archie momentarily renders most of Bones' other comparatively reasonable explanations unconvincing and naïve. Archie's story bluntly contradicts the plain evidence at the close of Act I, when he coolly stage manages the slick and efficient dance routine in which the jumpers dispose of McFee's body in a plastic bag produced after the fashion of a circus magician from Archie's pocket. In this scenario, we again view Archie as a ruthlessly corrupt politician but here Archie's brilliant showmanship offers a frightening display of how the mechanistic efficiency of this Rad-Lib pragmatism puts Logical Positivism into practice in the real world. If philosophical arguments are, as Archie holds, merely disputes about the rules of the language game, then crime detection becomes a form of show business and politics a spectator sport. Archie plays each game with a technical skill unimpaired by any qualm about the meaning or value of the game being played. In order to ensure that Bones will turn a blind eye to the discrepancy between the evidence of McFee's death and Archie's report as coroner that McFee committed suicide, he offers Bones first the Chair of Divinity and then the more prestigious Chair of Logic. Archie conducts his bribery elegantly, certain that his offers will seem attractive in view of the fact that the police force will, under the new Rad-Lib government, be 'thinned out to a ceremonial front for the peace-keeping activities of the Army'. Shortly after this, Archie discovers Bones performing for Dotty's diversion a drag charade of *The African Queen* and coolly blackmails Bones into dropping his criminal investigation. The connotations of political dictatorship which have already accumulated around the figure of Archie are given comic force when he interrupts George's comparison of the ethical judgements of St Francis and a 'lunatic tyrant' from history like Hitler, Stalin or Nero. It is Archie himself who unblinkingly draws a comparison between himself as Vice Chancellor and these tyrants. Once again a perspective opened up by Bones' rather literal-minded criminal investigation has political ramifications far beyond Bones' own comprehension. Has the pastiche whodunnit become a somewhat unlikely political allegory about the rise of totalitarian dictatorship?

Fourth, Crouch's revelation to George that his secretary was having an affair with McFee and may have killed him on discovering that McFee had not been honest with her about the fact that he was married, is a final twist in the detective fiction scenario, a wonderfully droll joke, for she has been poker-faced throughout the main action of the play, apparently primly disapproving of George's eccentricity, notwithstanding the fact that she was the woman who had performed a striptease from a swinging chandelier at the previous night's party. This twist offers another interpretation of the 'human interest' angle of the story. It is a denouement of the type common in Hollywood B-movies of the 1930s and 40s when, after ninety minutes of narrative set in the steamy underbelly of a corrupt society, it is disclosed that the villain is the prim spinster lady who turns out to have been concealing a sex life as exotic as any of the glamorous heroines of the film. After moving about the study unaware that Crouch is at that moment busy in the hallway incriminating her, she turns around to reveal a blood-spattered white coat. Surely she must be the culprit?

But before this, Crouch has informed Archie that McFee's life was going through a crisis at the time of his death:

> It was the astronauts fighting on the moon that finally turned him, Sir. Henry, he said to me, Henry, I am giving philosophical respectability to a new pragmatism in public life, of which there have been many disturbing examples, both here and on the Moon. . . . I have seen the future, Henry, he said; and it's yellow. (pp. 70–1)

So, up to a point, Archie's grotesque suggestion of a positive motive for suicide is plausible. Crouch is a little less reductive in his interpretation of events than Bones, although, as a stock stage servant, he defers to his betters, presenting himself as straightforward and naïve, playing up his attitude of bewilderment and prompting Archie to remark, patronisingly, 'Unlike mystery novels, life does not guarantee a denouement; and if it came, how would one know whether to believe it?' (p. 72)

If this truism represents the ultimate rejection of the many banal and hackneyed interpretations of the action given so far, it is also quite possible that it is merely another sophisticated ploy on Archie's part to account for these features of the evidence which point to him as the culprit. Whatever the case, he persuades Crouch to act as caretaker chairman of the symposium so that he himself can take McFee's place in the actual debate. If this is a bribe it is nicely appropriate! After all, Crouch actually is a caretaker and he does dabble in philosophy as a hobby.

At the moment when in practice the Rad-Lib approach to life may appear the only feasible position to adopt, given the chaos of the stage events, the action reaches its climax in the one moment in which the audience incontrovertibly witnesses an onstage death and perceives who did it. George, having seen the blood on his secretary's coat and realising that it must have been spattered on to it from the top of the cupboard, climbs up to reach the top of the cupboard in order to retrieve the arrow he had accidentally shot in response to Dotty's cries in Act I. This is the awful moment when he discovers he has shot his pet hare, Thumper, by mistake.

> Holding Thumper up by the arrow, George puts his face against the fur. A single sob. He steps backwards, down . . . CRRRRRUNCH!!! He has stepped, fatally, on Pat. With one foot on the desk and one foot on Pat, George looks down, and then puts up his head and cries out, 'Dotty, Help! Murder!' (p. 72)

These are almost the same words Dotty had cried when George began dictating his paper in Act I. A clear parallel emerges between the death of McFee and the death of George's pets. While George has not been able to feel very much spontaneous grief on learning of McFee's death, he is bereft by the discovery that he is accidentally responsible for the killing of his pet hare and tortoise, regarding himself as a murderer. The moment is one of the funniest and most poignant in modern theatre. It returns us to the starting point of the play proper with a new insight into George and Dotty's inability to live up to the moral responsibilities

implied by the injunction to love thy neighbour. Earlier,
when faced with the corpse of McFee, Dotty's serious cries
for help were misinterpreted by George as neurotic attention-
seeking games – a self-pitying extension of her histrionic
stage personality into her private life. Now he collapses,
crying desperately for help, over the death of the pets he has
employed to illustrate his philosophical arguments. While we
are made poignantly aware of his genuine love for the pets,
we are also reminded comically of his inability to love and
sustain Dotty in marriage.

The pastiche whodunnit set in motion by Inspector Bones is
here both parodied and complemented by the interpretation
of an action parallel to that of McFee's murder – the killing
of George's pets. The irony inherent in the comparison
between the search for two culprits – the murderer of McFee
and the murderer of Thumper – suggests a further interpretation of the action of *Jumpers* as a well-made play presenting
a sophisticated, bittersweet view of George and Dotty's
descent from romantic bliss to domestic hell. This, of course,
is not the final view of events. The coda reassembles the
strands of the play into a final theatrical vaudeville which
further challenges the possibility of finding certainty in a
world whose appearance is so dazzlingly equivocal.

The coda presents George's nightmare vision of the Rad-
Lib philosophy in action. It recapitulates a number of the
gymnastic and show business images from the prologue
sequence to return the argument of the play to its starting
point. This time, however, the action seems to dissolve from
a philosophy symposium to a TV game show, a scene from
Star Trek, a murder trial, a High Church procession, a scene
from *Richard III*, the jumpers' display (with the new Archbishop shot out of the pyramid this time around), to climax
in Dotty's entrance on a spangled crescent moon so that she
finally receives a chance to perform the routine which she
flunked in the prologue. It is as though all the major images
of the play, both verbal and visual, have been reduced to
the terms of a single perspective in which murder is shown
by Archie as justifiable according to the conventions of popular entertainment to which the institutions of religion, learning, government or law have been reduced.

A final frozen tableau is held as George and Archie recapitulate their philosophical positions. George's carefully structured arguments gradually disintegrate into a desperate parody of learned discourse which deliberately echoes Lucky's speech in *Waiting for Godot*:

> A remarkable number of apparently intelligent people are baffled by the fact that a different group of apparently intelligent people profess to a knowledge of God when common sense tells *them* – the first group of intelligent people – that knowledge is only a possibility in matters that can be demonstrated to be true or false.... And yet ... these same people ... will, nevertheless, and without any sense of inconsistency claim to *know* that life is better than death, that love is better than hate, and that the light shining through the east window of this bloody gymnasium is more beautiful than a rotting corpse! – In evidence of which I ask you, gentlemen of the jury, to consider the testimony of such witnesses as Zeno Evil, St Thomas Augustine, Jesus Moore and my late friend the late Herr Thumper who was as innocent as a rainbow. (pp. 77–8)

George's true love for his pets is evident in the poetic rhythm and idiom of the last lines, suggesting that whether or not it can be *logically* demonstrated, love or faith constitutes some sort of proof of the existence of God and of moral absolutes. Archie's final speech is a stock pastiche of the Beckettian mode but there is a grim irony in his cynical misuse of the characteristic stoicism evinced by Beckett to justify Archie's glib substitution of technology for religion, morality and logic:

> Do not despair – many are happy much of the time; more eat than starve, more are healthy than sick, more curable than dying; not so many dying as dead; and one of the thieves was saved ... millions of children grow up without suffering deprivation, and millions, while deprived and cruelly treated, none the less grow up. No laughter is sad and many tears are joyful. At the graveside the undertaker doffs his top hat and impregnates the prettiest mourner. (p. 78)

His last line ('Wham, bam, thank you Sam') both

acknowledges Beckett and returns the play, full circle, to its beginning. As Dotty reiterates the play's overall presentation of contemporary humanity's fall from grace in her unaccompanied singing ('Goodbye spooney, Juney Moon'), it is paradoxical that in the context of Stoppard's presentation of logical arguments a popular entertainment form has acquired philosophical significance.

The Real Thing

5   STOPPARD AND THE CRITICS

The National Theatre production of *Jumpers* established Tom Stoppard's reputation as arguably the most important writer of serious comedy to have emerged in Britain since the Second World War. His next full-length play after *Jumpers* was *Travesties*. In it Stoppard seemed to combine the two most striking features of *Rosencrantz And Guildenstern Are Dead* and *Jumpers*: metadrama and complex philosophical debate. In creating a dialectical play out of the conflicting ideas of Lenin, James Joyce and Tristan Tzara (the eccentric Dada artist), Stoppard at the same time managed to cast two of these famous revolutionary figures as characters in an amateur performance of Oscar Wilde's *The Importance of Being Earnest* – a performance which did actually take place in Zurich in 1916. By means of the device of filtering actual history through the somewhat unreliable memory of Henry Carr, a minor British consular official in Zurich during the First World War, Stoppard typically set up a double theatrical perspective. From one point of view, all the historical events in *Travesties* are moments somewhat inaccurately recalled in the form of scenes from a production of Wilde's well-known farce. Most of the action set in 1916 echoes, in terms of both verbal and behavioural performance, the upper class dandyism which Wilde employs to mock his straitlaced and hypocritical society. But the underlying framework of events is historically accurate and Stoppard is conscientious in his attempt to express through the characters of Lenin,

James Joyce and Tristan Tzara the intellectual perspective of each.

Stoppard's characteristic refusal to resolve the dialectical tension between art and history gave rise to a series of criticisms by reviewers and scholars who had praised Stoppard's other work highly. Much of the criticism suggested that the development of plot in *Travesties* had no necessary relationship to the outcome of the characters' destinies: as Ronald Hayman has said in his early critical study of the plays, there is no internal dynamic in *Travesties*. Kenneth Tynan, the great theatre journalist and literary manager of the National Theatre, said of the famous scene between James Joyce and Tristan Tzara – a travesty of the scene between Lady Bracknell and John Worthing in Wilde's play, which at the same time recalls a chapter of Joyce's *Ulysses* – that it was 'like a triple-decker bus going nowhere'. Charges of intellectual shallowness and cleverness for its own sake had been levelled at *Rosencrantz and Guildenstern Are Dead* but, from this point in his career, it became more and more the fashion for critics to attack Stoppard for presenting a circus of facile intellectual and theatrical tricks, thus oversimplifying or side-stepping serious issues.

His next play, *Dirty Linen*, written for Ed Berman and presented at the Almost Free Theatre in 1976, might seem to be a mocking rejoinder to his critics' earnestness. This 'knickers farce' about sexual misconduct in the House of Commons brilliantly shows off Stoppard's 'cheap side' once more. As a seeming riposte to the complaints that he was unable to engage seriously with important contemporary issues, Stoppard in 1977 produced *Every Good Boy Deserves Favour*, a theatre piece with music by André Previn. Michael Billington wittily commented in the *Guardian* (26 June 1982) that 'Stoppard brilliantly defies the theatrical law that says you cannot have your hand on your heart and your tongue in your cheek at the same time', illuminating the typically Stoppardian strategy of expressing a serious subject in the form of a theatrical (in this case theatrical *and* musical) game. In choosing to write about the abuse of psychiatric medicine to brainwash political dissidents in the Soviet Union, Stoppard may have been attempting to prove to his

critics that he was able to employ his indisputable theatrical
skills for the treatment of important contemporary issues,
while at the same time rejecting the easy assumption that
witty verbal and visual comedy or metatheatrical game-
playing are forms inappropriate for expressing serious social
and political concerns.

Although *Every Good Boy Deserves Favour* was hailed by
many critics as an artistic triumph, Stoppard nevertheless
continued to be reprimanded for his apparent unwillingness
to move beyond a contrived and shallow formalism, and for
consequently failing in the theatre to engage the feelings
of his audience. These criticisms were often vaguely associated with Stoppard's self-confessed dislike of naturalistic
theatre, while his alleged inability to create convincing
female characters was taken as another sign of artistic
immaturity.

In September 1977, Stoppard appeared to succeed tri-
umphantly in confounding his critics by creating a play for
BBC television which employed the more-or-less naturalistic
conventions of television drama at the same time as it played
the intellectual games characteristic of his most exhilarating
stage plays. The reason Stoppard gave for his apparent
change of style was eminently practical.

> *Professional Foul* had to be realistic . . . because . . . the effec-
> tiveness of dangerous theatrical devices on the stage depends
> on them being difficult to do in the physical situation you are
> working in. Once you have a camera and editing facilities, I
> lose all interest in trying to astonish people by what actually
> happens, because anything *can*.
>
> (*Guardian*, July 1979)

Apart from throwing light on the construction of *Jumpers*
and *Travesties* as quintessentially theatrical events, this gives
some indication of Stoppard's sensitivity to his chosen
medium. *Professional Foul* can loosely be described as a naturalistic reworking of the ethical debate in *Jumpers* in which
the Professor of Moral Philosophy is actually brought face to
face with the implications of his thesis about the relationship
between abstract moral principles and particular historical
actions. When Anderson, the Cambridge don, is confronted

with the mother and child of an ex-student who is being victimised by the Czech government on dubious political grounds, he is forced to set aside his usual philosophical scruples about committing any dishonest action in order to smuggle his ex-student's manuscript out of the country, thus defying the state's restrictions on freedom of expression. The play's interweaving of thematically parallel plots concerning a philosophy colloquium, an international football test match and the intolerable oppression suffered by the Hollar family, cleverly focuses all aspects of the debate concerning ethical and unethical behaviour by means of the metaphor of the professional foul (in football parlance, an offence deliberately committed to achieve a desired objective).

When *Night and Day* was set to open in November 1978, critics wondered whether Stoppard's new-found social and political commitment would influence the shape and content of this new stage play, his first attempt to write explicitly about love. It was also the first production of a Stoppard play to originate in a large West End theatre, a sign that his reputation had been transformed from that of a young and experimental dramatist of ideas to that of an established and serious commercial playwright. *Night and Day* was also Stoppard's first play to contain a female character whose role was unquestionably the central one. While the play was by no means universally acclaimed by the critics it became a huge commercial success, running for two years at the Phoenix Theatre with three star actresses (first Diana Rigg, then Maggie Smith, who was replaced in London by Susan Hampshire when she left to perform the role on Broadway).

With *Night and Day* Stoppard consciously attempted to prove that he could write a well-made play about two 'serious' subjects – love and the ethics of newspaper journalism. By dramatising in detail Ruth Carson's conflicting feelings for a husband whom she cannot fully love and two journalists, one of whom she has recently slept with and the other to whom she feels physically attracted, and at the same time conducting a debate about press freedom, Stoppard intended the play to be 'realistic' without entirely sacrificing the witty dialectic of action and argument characteristic of his earlier 'humming bird' plays. Ironically, many critics saw fit to express their regret that Stoppard had given up writing brilliant theatrical and comic tours-de-force such as *Jumpers* and *Travesties*: some assumed that he may have been lured by the financial rewards of the commercial theatre to forsake the high-altitude theatrical and intellectual virtuosity which had become his trademark.

The Real Thing was his next original, full-length stage play. Partly because it comes closer to being autobiographical than any other play that Stoppard has written, it also appears to constitute a complex response to much of the criticism levelled against his plays over the eight years since *Travesties* had first been performed. One might assume that Stoppard had set himself three challenges:

1. To prove that he was capable of writing a 'serious' commercial play.
2. To prove that he was capable of writing an erudite and witty comedy that dealt passionately with personal relationships.
3. To produce an answer to the charge that his writing was right-wing and elitist, of interest only to a middle class audience and insensitive to the broader issues of social and political life in Britain in the 1970s and 1980s.

6   LOVE OF ART AND THE ART OF LOVE

It is probably true to say that Stoppard did not manage to defend his political standpoint as coherently as his critics thought was necessary. But *The Real Thing* does constitute a complex statement about aspects of private experience which deeply concern Stoppard. By integrating his intellectually sophisticated and characteristically playful comic strategy with the format of the West End play, *The Real Thing* affirmed Stoppard's commitment to the values of personal morality above the demands of public action in the political sphere. *The Real Thing* casts a playwright as hero. The play examines why Henry (the playwright) cannot write about love – which is Stoppard's way of writing about love. By confronting and rationalising his own alleged failings as a youthful playwright Stoppard on one level manages to overcome them, and ironically to refute the suggestion that it is necessary for a mature contemporary dramatist to deal directly with private emotions.

More so than *Night and Day*, *The Real Thing* powerfully expresses Stoppard's post-modernist perception that it is impossible to write first-hand about lived experience because an individual's experience is always mediated by the forms of a particular culture. It is significant that Stoppard returns to the technique of metadrama which had given him a major breakthrough as a playwright in *Rosencrantz And Guildenstern Are Dead*. Having experimented with realistic theatre conventions in *Night and Day* and pushed his abstract formalist technique as far as it would go in *Travesties, Dogg's Hamlet* and *Every Good Boy Deserves Favour*, he returned to his dramaturgical middle ground. In *Rosencrantz and Guildenstern Are Dead*, he had situated the world view of Shakespeare within a perspective provided by *Waiting for Godot* in order to locate the world of his audience in the tension between these two constructions of reality. In *The Real Thing*, Stoppard obliquely illuminates the common experience of love as a cliché of everyday life by contrasting the tragic or pathetic view of love in plays from the classical repertoire (his allusions are to plays by Ford, Strindberg and Chekhov) with the more mundane view of love reflected in such a well-made West End play as *House of Cards*, written by Stoppard's alter ego character, Henry.

The problem of identifying 'the real thing' (what love is) is posed in the form of a series of theatrical puzzles about the distinction between the dramatic action of *The Real Thing* and the plays-within-the-play. The opening scene, with its somewhat stilted presentation of marital infidelity, is contrasted with the ensuing scene, in which three actors and a writer talk as cleverly as the characters in Noel Coward's *Private Lives* while beneath the brittle surface of the banter it is apparent that two marriages are breaking up. When it dawns on an audience that the opening is a scene from *House of Cards* and that the portrayal of the fictional world of *The Real Thing* properly begins in Scene 2, it is perceived that actual experience may appear as clichéd and social behaviour as contrived as they are in well-made plays. Stoppard introduces the other view of love as an heroic but destructive passion (also a type of cliché) by quoting moments from a number of plays which are being rehearsed at various points in *The Real Thing* by Annie, who has by Scene 4 become Henry's second wife. These plays seem to Henry to succeed in directly articulating those passionate feelings which he believes he is unable to express as a playwright.

So we have a further perspective on the well-made play Stoppard is apparently writing about a writer of well-made plays. The view of love embodied in these classics challenges the reticence of the typical well-made play and directly evokes the dark and subterranean passions Henry is unable to dramatise and which we later realise he has been ignoring or repressing in his own relationships. Stoppard had created the text of *Rosencrantz and Guildenstern Are Dead* by improvising actors' subtexts for the minor characters in *Hamlet*. In *The Real Thing* he devises a well-made play as a metadramatic comment on his own well-made play, creating a dialectic between play and metaplay, text and subtext, conscious and subconscious, the clearly stated and the implied. Thus *The Real Thing* articulates an explicit discourse on the relationship between drama and reality whereas the typical well-made play, in order to maintain the naturalistic illusion of a 'slice of life', must repress such discourse. In writing a play about the difficulties of writing about love, Stoppard achieves what Henry says he cannot do as a playwright which is to 'write love'.

Ironically, Stoppard's paradoxical achievement in writing about love may have been the fundamental reason for the play's commercial success. In deconstructing the well-made West End play, Stoppard at the same time succeeds in writing a highly sophisticated one. Act I of *The Real Thing* establishes the central dialectic: by means of an artful arrangement of scenes, reality and theatricality are shown to be on the one hand continuous and on the other opposed.

Each scene is carefully contrasted with the one preceding it to focus on the characters' modes of expressing their emotions. In order to ask the question 'What is the real thing?' (i.e. love) Stoppard must necessarily ask what are the rules of the well-made play which traditionally reflects the bourgeois conception of love. (An analysis of love in a middle class milieu is tantamount to an analysis of the bourgeois art forms which have traditionally expressed it.) This is why *The Real Thing* begins with the scene from *House of Cards* – precisely the kind of play which an audience would expect as the vehicle for the presentation of love among the architect classes.

The second scene (in which the 'real' action of *The Real Thing* begins) appears for a while to exist entirely within the fictional world of *House of Cards*, so that initially *The Real Thing* provokes an awareness that the experience of a passionate relationship actually does lead to the kind of complications which are the clichés of a well-made plot. The irony inherent in Stoppard's play is that an investigation of what constitutes true fidelity in a passionate relationship provokes Max in Scene 3 and Henry in Scenes 9 and 10 to behave in as clichéd a manner as the cuckolded husband Max plays in *House of Cards*. The implication is that what makes a loving relationship unique is a kind of mystery which can only be comprehended through the experience of its absence. The status quo at the beginning of *The Real Thing* is a shallow and conventional existence in which the characters experience the comfortable emotions and behave with the trite sophistication which in a well-made play constitutes the norm of middle class behaviour. Even Max's pain on discovering in Scene 3 that Henry and Annie are having an affair is acceptable as an element within the typical scenario of a sophisticated West End play. Stoppard takes care not to permit the audience to empathise too fully with Max, who does not actually appear in the play after the moment at the end of Scene 3 when his cries of anguish are overtaken by music.

At the end of Act I, Henry and Annie are both quite smug about their relationship, in spite of their sophisticated honesty about the possibility that Henry might be seduced by one of his actress friends and that Annie might be campaigning to have the young soldier Brodie released from prison because she is attracted to him.

> HENRY: I love love. I love having a lover and being one. The insularity of passion. I love it. I love the way it blurs the distinction between everyone who isn't one's lover. Only two kinds of presence in the word. There's you and there's them. I love you so.
> ANNIE: I love you so, Hen. (*They kiss. The alarm on Henry's wristwatch goes off. They separate.*)
>
> (p. 44)

This image of the comfortable bliss of a middle class couple is somewhat undercut by Annie's action when, left alone on stage a few seconds later, she begins to search Henry's private papers, which reminds the audience both of the way the architect played by Max in *House of Cards* had discovered his wife's passport when she was supposed to be in Switzerland and of Max's discovery of Annie's infidelity when he finds Henry's soiled handkerchief in her car.

The first scene of Act II (Scene 5) presents an argument between Henry and Annie about the merits of the play written by the young soldier who has been jailed for setting fire to a wreath on the Cenotaph. This articulates the central dialectic between authentic and inauthentic experience in terms of an explicit debate about 'real' and ersatz literature. From this moment in the play, action and philosophical argument are interwoven with metadramatic scenes to develop the central dialectic so that it becomes more self-reflexive and more complex.

Annie's main point is that the subject matter of Brodie's left-wing political play gives it importance as art. In spite of its linguistic and structural clumsiness, Annie maintains that it is valuable, both because Brodie has used his actual experience as the basis for his play and because it constitutes a passionate protest against an unjust social and political status quo.

> ANNIE: He's not a writer. He's a convict. *You're* a writer. You write *because* you're a writer. Even when you write *about* something, you have to think up something to

> write about just so you can keep writing. More well-
> chosen words nicely put together. . . . Then somebody
> who isn't in on the game comes along, like Brodie,
> who really has something to write about, something
> real, and you can't get through it. Well, *he* couldn't
> get through *yours*, so where are you? To you, he can't
> write. To him write is all you *can* do.
>
> (p. 51)

Henry's argument rests on the idea that the seriousness
of a play's subject matter, or the authenticity of the experience which lies behind it, is irrelevant to its artistic merits.
Its significance as art depends on the writer's skill in manipulating the structural properties of the medium. He uses the
example of a cricket bat to illustrate this point.

> This thing here, which looks like a wooden club, is actually
> several pieces of particular wood cunningly put together in a
> certain way so that the whole thing is sprung, like a dance
> floor. It's for hitting cricket balls with. If you get it right, the
> cricket ball will travel two hundred yards in four seconds,
> and all you've done is give it a knock like knocking the top
> off a bottle of stout, and it makes a noise like a trout taking
> a fly. . . . (*He clucks his tongue to make the noise.*) What we're
> trying to do is to write cricket bats, so that when we throw
> up an idea and give it a little knock, it might . . . *travel* . . .
>
> (p. 52)

The ramifications of this argument are revealed in a series
of debates in Scenes 6, 7 and 9. In Scene 6, Billy, the young
actor playing Giovanni to Annie's Annabella in *'Tis Pity
She's a Whore*, turns Annie's earlier argument against her, as
she turns Henry's earlier argument against Billy. Even
though Billy does not think Brodie's play is well written (in
fact the scene starts with Billy parodying the scene in Brodie's play in which the soldier and the woman meet on a
train), he demonstrates the validity of Brodie's political perspective in an argument about the class system. Annie
adopts Henry's thesis about words being neutral, and political and ethical concepts being mental constructs which do
not refer directly to things in the material world. 'There's no
system. People group together when they've got something in

common. . . . There's nothing really *there* – it's just the way
you see it. Your perception' (pp. 57–8). Billy's materialist
perspective is akin to that of Brodie as he says, 'I prefer
Brodie. He sounds like rubbish but you know he's right.
You sound all right, but you know it's rubbish' (p. 58).

The notion that reality is constructed by the subjective
consciousness of the individual is playfully illustrated in the
argument in Scene 7 between Henry and his daughter
Debbie about the compatibility of free love with fidelity.
Each term reflects quite clearly the value system of the
character who uses it and is further elaborated in the difference between Henry's understanding and that of his ex-wife
Charlotte concerning the nature of marriage.

> HENRY: I thought we'd made a commitment.
> CHARLOTTE: There are no commitments. Only bargains. . . .
>   You're an idiot. *Were* an idiot.
>
> (p. 65)

At this point Charlotte is in fact using Henry's description
as developed in the argument in Scene 5 of the way values
are constructed according to the individual's existential perspective. In rejecting Brodie's dogmatic insistence that objective reality reflects his own simplistic left-wing views ('war
is profit, politicians are puppets, parliament is a farce, justice
is a fraud, property is theft . . .') Henry says:

> politics, justice, patriotism – they aren't . . . like coffee mugs.
> There's nothing real there – separate from our perception of
> them. So if you try to change them as though there were
> something there to change, you'll get frustrated and frus-
> tration will finally make you violent. If you know this and
> proceed with humility, you may perhaps alter people's percep-
> tions so that they behave a little differently at that axis of
> behaviour where we locate politics or justice; but if you don't
> know this, then you're acting on a mistake.
>
> (pp. 53–4)

Typically, Stoppard foreshadows Henry's agony throughout the second half of the play over the question of Annie's
adultery with Billy. The question of what constitutes fidelity

(the difference between a commitment and a bargain) is formulated and reformulated in various contexts in the play. This provides a series of frameworks each of which a member of the audience might adopt in turn when attempting to comprehend the value of Henry and Annie's love for each other. Annie's commitment to Brodie is established in Scene 2 and motivates an exchange at the end of Scene 4 about the difference between a criminal action and a political gesture:

> ANNIE: Arson is burning down buildings. Setting fire to the wreath on the Cenotaph is a symbolic act.
>
> (p. 43)

Henry's lack of jealousy about her involvement with other men perplexes and irritates Annie because it seems to indicate a lack of depth in his feelings for her. Her 'relationship' with Brodie does become problematic for Henry in Scene 5 when, after their first full-scale row over the political/artistic significance of Brodie's play, Henry makes an accusation to which Annie responds in a way that suggests there may be deep tensions underlying the affection they have so far expressed towards each other:

> HENRY: (*Exasperated*) *Why Brodie?* Do you fancy him or what? (*She looks back at him and he sees that he has made a mistake*) I take it back.
>
> ANNIE: Too late. (*She leaves the room*).
>
> (p. 55)

Having primed an audience to watch for any signs that Annie is having a relationship with Brodie, Stoppard immediately follows this with a scene on a train (Scene 6) which appears to be a flashback to Annie's first meeting with Brodie until, after thirty seconds or so, it turns out that Billy (the actor playing Giovanni in *'Tis Pity She's a Whore*) is sending up the dialogue from Brodie's play (Annie had asked him to read the play with a view to helping her put it on). The irony is that Billy's flirtation with Annie constitutes the only real threat to her relationship with Henry. At the end of the play, Annie's commitment to Brodie is explained: she reveals that he was infatuated by her TV persona. Apparently her guilt at not being able to reciprocate his feelings was the real motivation for the passionate sponsorship of his cause:

> He was helpless, like a three-legged calf, nervous as anything. A boy on the train chatting me up. . . . By the time we got to London he would have followed me into the Ku Klux Klan. He tagged on. . . . And when we were passing the war memorial he got his lighter out. . . . Private Brodie goes over the top to the slaughter, not an idea in his head except to impress me. What else could I do? He was my recruit.
>
> (p. 80)

Underlying the action of Act II is not only the question of whether Annie's love for Henry will be replaced by her attraction to Brodie but also the question of whether she *is* in fact attracted to Brodie and, from Scene 6 onwards, the additional possibility that she might succumb to the romantic overtures of Billy – potentially a middle class surrogate for Brodie, whom he portrays in the teleplay. Henry's suspicious jealousy about Annie and Billy initiates a profound change in his attitude to love. In Scene 10 Henry himself provides the first explicit articulation of the idea implicit in Annie's sense (expressed in Scene 4) that his lack of jealousy somehow signifies an absence of real passion:

> I don't believe in behaving well. I don't believe in debonair relationships. . . . I believe in mess, tears, pain, self-abasement, loss of self-respect, nakedness. Not caring doesn't seem much different from not loving.
>
> (p. 72)

Henry begins to experience 'the real thing' once he has started to behave as the stereotypical jealous husband Stoppard has twice before presented to the audience (Max's character in Scene 1 and Max himself in Scene 3). The last phase in the process of Henry's maturity brings him to an acceptance in Scenes 12 and 13 of the fact that he cannot possess Annie totally, that each individual must retain some independence outside the relationship in order to preserve the integrity of the relationship itself.

The argument in *The Real Thing* about the nature of passionate relationships subsumes the argument over Brodie's political viewpoint. The revelation of Annie's feelings of guilt over the fact that she could neither reciprocate Brodie's feelings for her nor match the naïve gesture calculated to impress her which had led to his imprisonment, constitutes a complicated proof of her fidelity to Henry. Stoppard's caricature of Brodie as an ungrateful oaf presents a gross oversimplification of the political argument elaborated in Scene 5, but it does provide an opportunity to demonstrate that the relationship between Henry and Annie can encompass her relationship with Billy (which at this point she declares to be over) and her misplaced liberal guilt about Brodie. This scene represents Stoppard's contrived theatrical demonstration of the aphorism that 'public postures have the configuration of private derangement'. As a revelation of Annie's particular form of liberal neurosis, the scene is witty and powerful: as a serious attempt to conclude the debate between materialist and idealist perspectives on society and politics it is extremely simplistic and exhibits the kind of prejudice Henry himself warns Annie against in Scene 5.

Notwithstanding the play's reductive implication at this moment, *The Real Thing* is immensely sophisticated and thought-provoking. Stoppard proves himself to be one of the very few contemporary writers capable of using the well-made play format as a vehicle for wide-ranging philosophical discourse on the passions which engage people in romantic relationships, in art and in politics.

PART TWO: PERFORMANCE

Rosencrantz and Guildenstern Are Dead – Old Vic, 1967

7 CREATING THE WORLD OF THE PLAY: SETS, COSTUMES AND EFFECTS

Even those critics who professed to find the play shallow were impressed by the sheer theatricality of the entertainment offered by the National Theatre at the Old Vic on the evening of Tuesday, 11 April 1967. Perhaps the most remarkable feature of Derek Goldby's production was the way in which it created an impression of an archetypical *Hamlet* world, a distillation of all the productions within living memory into a Victorian-Gothic atmosphere which emblematised every playgoer's sensory impression of Shakespeare's Elsinore, even at those points where Stoppard's play departs most radically from Shakespeare's text. Members of the audience arriving for the opening performance were well aware of the status of the Old Vic, as the home of Shakespeare and classical drama in London. The joke of the play's title was immediately apparent on various levels. Theatregoers had witnessed a number of great productions of *Hamlet* at the Old Vic. John Gielgud had played it a few times in the 1920s and 30s, Laurence Olivier in 1937 and Peter O'Toole in 1963. In fact O'Toole's *Hamlet* was the production chosen by Olivier to inaugurate the first season of the National Theatre at the Old Vic in 1963. The death of Rosencrantz and Guildenstern had been reported numerous times on the stage of the Old Vic and some members of the audience may have been aware of a further irony if they were able to recall that Olivier (the Director of the National Theatre) had cut Rosencrantz and Guildenstern from his film version of *Hamlet* in 1948.

Now two minor characters in the play were making a star

appearance at the home of Shakespeare, shortly after their successful debut at the Edinburgh Festival in a play by an unknown playwright. Undoubtedly, one of the surprising and witty aspects of the Old Vic production was the fact of this play's performance at this particular theatre. From their first glimpse of the setting at the start of the performance, spectators were reminded of the tradition of Shakespeare production that Stoppard himself is playing with.

The setting of the production, together with the costumes, props and lighting, established from the outset the all-purpose 'stage-Elizabethan' environment which constitutes the world of Stoppard's play, a somewhat unreal location redolent of Olivier's moody monochromatic film or of countless theatre productions with their stark sets of platforms and velvet drapes, their vaguely Gothic archways, medieval tapestries and vaguely Elizabethan costumes. Because this is a 'play-within-or-beneath-the-play-*Hamlet*', its setting must make reference to all the most popular visual clichés associated with *Hamlet*. One of the conventions which has arisen in the twentieth century for the production of Shakespeare is the non-illusionistic multipurpose setting. Since the Shakespeare productions of Granville-Barker at the Savoy before the First World War, modern designers have rejected the detailed realistic settings of their nineteenth-century predecessors with their complex scene changes in favour of more abstract arrangements of rostra, flights of stairs and curtains, at times utilising a revolving stage to carry the relationship of the basic elements.

Desmond Heeley's setting for *Rosencrantz and Guildenstern Are Dead* exploited these basic principles, adding one or two tongue-in-cheek details to actualise Stoppard's opening stage direction: '*Two Elizabethans, passing the time in a place without any visible character*'. In fact, the atmosphere of the setting is just a little too self-consciously theatrical: it advertises its own effectiveness as a neutral background for Shakespeare's play, its Gothic atmosphere archly overstated, the artfulness of the scenic transformations just a little too slick to seem entirely probable.

Peter Lewis, writing in the *Daily Mail*, remarked that 'The production comes out of the dark like a spotlit jewel, full of vibrations' (12 April 1967), and other critics commented on the effectiveness of Richard Pilbrow's lighting. It is rare for reviewers actually to mention the lighting and this reflects something of the patina of theatricality with which the production aimed to gloss the play. The lighting designer employed a number of colour effects which effectively marked the changes of scene that Stoppard implies in the text, without causing any break in the flow of the action.

In addition to two curved intersecting rostra which provided various levels upon which actors could stand, there were three backcloths painted in perspective to suggest different locations within and outside the castle, and the sail of a seventeenth-century ship. These were placed behind a gauze cloth which rendered them invisible under certain lighting states so that one could be flown out and another flown in to create smooth scene changes at various points in the play. There was a revolving stage which could be used to change the position of the rostrum and the props included a cart for the troupe of travelling players which contained a chest, masks and various other odd handprops evoking the tricks of their trade, and four large barrels and a deck chair to complement the backcloth of the sail in evoking the deck of a ship. The short list of props in the stage manager's prompt book reinforces the impression that the stage was a sparsely furnished 'wooden O' representative of a modern view of the theatre of Shakespeare's time as one in which scenes can be conjured up in the minds of the audience with the aid of poetic language and skilful acting. This was indeed the great achievement of the production. It capitalised on the twentieth-century tradition of simple, non-illusionistic decor for Shakespeare, stressing the power of the imagination to transform the bare boards of the stage from one location into another. But its simple settings were also very cleverly designed in conjunction with stylish conventionalised Elizabethan costumes and the vividly theatrical lighting to promote the National Theatre's reputation for a paradoxically minimalist kind of total theatre, as exemplified three years earlier in John Dexter's spectacular production of Peter Shaffer's *The Royal Hunt of the Sun*, with its bare stage brilliantly metamorphosed into the mountains of the

Andes by a few dozen actors miming the Spanish conquest of Peru in a series of inventive stylised movement sequences.

The ability of Desmond Heeley's simple arrangement of rostra and backcloths to suggest with the aid of lighting and sound effects the interior of a Gothic castle, the open countryside and the deck of a ship, while remaining clearly recognisable as a functional wooden structure, emphasised the role of the actors and the discourse on acting which constitutes the major theme of *Rosencrantz and Guildenstern Are Dead*.

8   STYLES OF ACTING: ACTORS ON THE ART OF BEING

The first moments of the play might register as a clever staging trick, the colloquial 1960s style creating a frisson in the theatre. In place of the conventional opening of *Hamlet* with the hushed entrance of Marcellus and Bernardo waiting on the battlements of Elsinore at dead of night for the appearance of the ghost, the director has chosen to show two court attendants spinning coins to pass away the time. Is this, a spectator might ask, yet another trendy, iconoclastic interpretation designed to demonstrate that Shakespeare is our contemporary?

After a few moments of silent action, however, the dead-pan figures start to speak. The first shock of the evening is to hear these two Elizabethans, the stockier one in brown, the other in peacock blue, speaking contemporary prose. Regular Old Vic first nighters would have recognised the first to speak as John Stride, already fairly well known for playing youthful roles in National Theatre productions. The other actor (Edward Petherbridge) would not really have been known by name to the audience, although some might remember having seen him in small roles.

The actors are sitting on the steps of the semi-circular wooden rostrum at each end of which a flight of three wide steps descends to the ground on either side of the centre point of the stage. The positioning of these figures dressed in doublet and hose involves a break in the usual decorum of Shakespearean staging. Minor characters in performances of the tragedies are usually deployed about the stage in quite stiff, formal groupings, as they stand to await instructions from the king and respond with polite ceremony to questions or commands. The play's first and characteristic visual joke implies a more casual, less rigidly choreographed mode of behaviour for these two minor characters while they are alone. Whereas in the court scenes they take their habitual place in the formal tableaux of court ceremonies, most of their life consists of waiting to be summoned to participate in these ceremonies.

Throughout the play, one of these actors repeats a version of the events which initiated their journey to the court of Elsinore:

ROS: . . . You remember that – this man woke us up.
GUIL: Yes.
ROS: We were sent for.
GUIL: Yes.
ROS: That's why we're here. . . . It was urgent – a matter of extreme urgency, a royal summons, his very words: official business and no questions asked.

(p. 14)

If they experience court life as a mechanical performance in rather limited roles, the time in between each particular appearance at court is devoid of purpose and filled with the anxiety of never knowing when or why they are going to be summoned to a scene of authentic action.

To observe Rosencrantz and Guildenstern sitting on the steps of a typical *Hamlet* set spinning coins which always come up 'heads' is immediately to grasp the central conceit of Stoppard's play. At the Old Vic, the joke was doubly funny as it confronted the audience with two young actors, Stride and Petherbridge, in the process of graduating from juvenile or supporting roles such as Rosencrantz and Guildenstern in Shakespeare's tragedy to star parts. Most supporting actors in a Shakespeare play spend the large part of the performance in their dressing rooms finding ways of occupying time between one short appearance and the next. At one level, Stoppard's play jokingly exploits the audience's recognition of this onstage-backstage dichotomy. Instead of a public scene in *Hamlet* to which an Old Vic audience would respond with the familiarity born of long acquaintance, the audience was made to witness what looked like the backstage life of two young actors waiting out the progress of *Hamlet* until they hear their first cue. From the outset the decorum of the setting was undercut by the casual 1960s attitude of the two young men lounging on the steps spinning coins.

Stride and Petherbridge played Rosencrantz and Guilden-stern as a sort of undergraduate double act, following Stop-pard's wry treatment of the information given in *Hamlet* that the two have been Hamlet's college companions at the University of Wittenberg. John Stride (Rosencrantz) had a somewhat cherubic face: by 1967 playgoers were accustomed to seeing him play 'straight' juveniles, fresh-faced sincere young men such as Romeo (Stratford, 1960), Fortinbras, Dunois in *St Joan* and Swiss Cheese, Mother Courage's naïve son. By contrast, Edward Petherbridge (Guildenstern) was something of an enigma: since 1964 he had played only small parts at the Old Vic and this fact was exploited by casting him as Guildenstern, his face and voice familiar to regular theatregoers but his personality somewhat unfathom-able. Guildenstern is an intellectual type. Petherbridge's voice had a gentle yet insinuating tone, his speech rhythms suggested the earnest perseverance of an intelligent under-graduate, but also sounded resigned and helpless at those moments when Stride's bluff puppy-dog innocence gave way to the anguished bafflement of the simpleton.

The opening business of spinning coins established a relationship of familiarity with the audience, who were immediately drawn into the suspense as the coin came up 'heads' five times before the tension was dissolved. A tone of jokey self-consciousness which makes implicit reference to the audience was established by Guildenstern's 'There is an art to the building up of suspense', Stoppard wittily indicat-ing both the onstage suspense and that of the audience waiting eagerly to grasp the exposition of the plot. This little sequence foreshadowed the dominant pattern of action which repeatedly emphasised the sense of coincidence or mystery inherent in the dramatic situation only to have its exaggerated portentousness ruptured either by the pathos of Guildenstern's immature philosophical speculations on possible explanations for their peculiar circumstances or by the intrusion of a major, though usually inexplicable, twist of the *Hamlet* plot.

The positioning of the actors facing 'out front' towards the audience, underlined an inherent feature of the dialogue which made these two figures the channel through which the spectator's attitude to the action was focused. Rosencrantz and Guildenstern became representative of the audience, encouraging them to experience directly the characters' perplexity at the seeming inconsistencies and absurdities of the *Hamlet* plot, a plot which most members of the audience knew before they entered the theatre. While Stride-Rosencrantz and Petherbridge-Guildenstern were actors in Stoppard's play, they made the audience complicit with them as they performed their role as an onstage audience to the action of *Hamlet*. A kind of black comedy was derived from the fact that the Old Vic audience knew what Rosencrantz and Guildenstern did not. Even those who did not know *Hamlet* would have realised from the outset that the two characters were doomed to die. ('There are wheels within wheels!') The more ingeniously Petherbridge's Guildenstern attempted to manufacture philosophical explanations and the more earnestly Stride's Rosencrantz tried to adopt obvious solutions to spurious problems the more the audience laughed at them for failing to make the obvious deductions from the available evidence.

Many reviewers of the first performance noticed the comic pathos of Stride and Petherbridge's characterisations. B. A. Young (*Financial Times*, 12 April 1967) said that 'they have given body to perfect vacuity'. Herbert Kretzmer (*Daily Express*, 12 April 1967) commented on 'their colourlessness, their ambiguity . . . their very ordinariness'. Peter Lewis (*Daily Mail*, 12 April 1967) developed this idea in his suggestion that 'in failing [to prove that their lives have meaning] . . . they come to stand for any of us, summoned we know not why to live in an Elsinore not of our choosing, playing the parts people expect of us, and watching death approach with incomprehension'.

Peter Lewis sensitively interpreted the relationship engendered between Stride-Rosencrantz and Petherbridge-Guildenstern and the audience. As the action progresses Rosencrantz and Guildenstern begin to appear more and more as spectators, not merely to the action of *Hamlet*, but to their own lives. The difference between the style of the two central performances and the playing of the other actors indicated this major theme. In fact, Stride and Petherbridge distinguished Rosencrantz from Guildenstern only in so far as performers in a comic double act in a revue or music hall sketch are characterised. Other than clearly outlining the characters' complementary and antithetical qualities they limited their performances to portraying the intensity of each character's anxiety. The two actors beautifully exploited their own youthfulness to suggest the earnestness of students whose immature attempt to probe the meaning of life before they have properly experienced it ironically prevents them from changing the rules of the game in which they are actually being manipulated as pawns. The two actors' sly handling of Stoppard's self-consciously witty text cleverly portrayed the manner in which people think aloud as a way of proving to themselves that they understand something they do not.

Characteristically, Rosencrantz and Guildenstern were discovered on stage as the play opened. (They do not do anything as decisive as making an entrance.) The first group of characters to make an entrance on to the Old Vic stage were the band of six travelling players, heralded by stock stage-Elizabethan music of pipes and drums. The acting and movement of this group was used to emphasise a theme which is signified in the text through the use of language which habitually describes action and character from an external behavioural perspective – as though the speakers perceived only the forms of objects and events and not their content or meaning. A good example of this occurs halfway through Act I when Guildenstern gives a second version of their summons to Elsinore: 'A man standing in his saddle in the half-lit half-alive dawn banged on the shutters and called two names. He was just a hat and a cloak levitating in the grey plume of his own breath.'

The appearance of the players on stage was a visual illustration of Stoppard's presentation of a world in which forms are devoid of content. The leader of the group, simply called 'the Player', is a cynical and bombastic actor. His narcissistic decadence was beautifully portrayed by Graham Crowden in a performance of studied self-mockery and sardonic malice. His slightly sinister manner implied that he might know more than he was letting on. From the outset the Player appeared to be acting; Crowden's performance was the stylistic antithesis to Stride's and Petherbridge's. Where they seemed to be improvising spontaneously, he gave a virtuoso exhibition of a well-practised routine. Where they were anxious to interpret the meaning of each fresh encounter, his every gesture signalled that he had seen it all before.

Graham Crowden had recently been a great success at the Old Vic as Augustus Colpoys, the old actor in Pinero's *Trelawney of the Wells*. His first entrance in Act I of *Rosencrantz and Guildenstern Are Dead* built upon the audience's recognition of this performer persona to create a bravura display of histrionic tricks. While revelling in his own rhetorical flourish, Crowden nevertheless conveyed the utter boredom of the jaded sensualist. With slightly whitened face, wearing multicoloured striped breeches and surrounded by his ragged troupe of down-at-heel thespians who illustrated his histrionic arias in the form of stylised dumb show, Crowden presented a symbol of the human being as actor. Whether the Player was performing a role or merely talking off the cuff, Crowden's manner hardly altered: if all the world's a stage then there is no moment when one is not acting.

GUIL: Well . . . aren't you going to change into your costume?
PLAYER: I never change out of it, Sir.
GUIL: Always in character.
PLAYER: That's it. (*Pause*)
GUIL: Aren't you going to – come *on*?
PLAYER: I *am* on.
GUIL: But if you *are* on, you can't *come* on. *Can* you?

PLAYER: I *start* on.
GUIL: But it hasn't *started*.

(p. 25)

On the one hand, the Player's slightly artificial style of speaking might have indicated the more formal speech of a middle-aged man (as opposed to the youthful 'mod' lingo of Rosencrantz and Guildenstern). On the other, it might have implied that every word and gesture had been pre-rehearsed, that every new encounter was not a spontaneous event but was in fact a pre-scripted performance which could only be executed according to well-known conventions, without the possibility of being improvised afresh.

The dichotomy of actor-spectator established by Stride and Petherbridge at this moment became the basis of a complex game whose rules appeared to change according to context:

PLAYER: I recognised you at once–
ROS: And who are we?
PLAYER: –as fellow artists.
ROS: I thought we were gentlemen.
PLAYER: For some of us it is performance, for others, patronage. They are two sides of the same coin, or, let us say, the same side of two coins. (*Bows again*) Don't clap too loudly – it's a very old world!
ROS: What is your line?
PLAYER: Tragedy, sir. Deaths and disclosures, universal and particular, denouements both unexpected and inexorable, transvestite melodrama on all levels including the suggestive. We transport you into a world of intrigue and illusion . . . clowns if you like, murderers – we can do you ghosts and battles, on the skirmish level, heroes, villains, tormented lovers – set pieces in the poetic vein; we can do you rapiers or rape or both, by all means, faithless wives and ravished virgins – flagrante delicto at a price, but that comes under realism for which there are special terms. . . . It costs little to watch and little more if you happen to get caught up in the action, if that's your taste and times being what they are.

(p. 17)

The speech seemed to echo the opening of the popular American musical *A Funny Thing Happened on the Way to the Forum* (London, 1964), by Stephen Sondheim and Burt Shevelove, in which Pseudolus the slave (played in the London production by Frankie Howerd) intersperses his listless singing of the number 'Comedy Tonight' with a deadpan introduction to the tawdry cast of type characters. The idea of portraying actors discussing and illustrating their craft within a play is by no means original. It occurs, of course, in *Hamlet,* but the notion of turning the tables on an audience and provoking a philosophical reflection on the relationship between acting and being, between theatrical and social role-playing, was most famously exploited by Pirandello who made the theme the basis for a series of plays written between 1916 and 1931. The device had been used by a succession of playwrights and became a stock-in-trade of the popular French dramatist Jean Anouilh, whose plays had been successful on the London stage during the 1950s and 1960s. In 1957 John Osborne had used onstage scenes from Edwardian music hall to mirror the decay of British society in *The Entertainer* and Joan Littlewood had staged her satirical exposé of the values and motives which promoted the First World War as a seaside pierrot show in *Oh What a Lovely War* (1964).

Stoppard exploited the resonances of this convention to create a metaphor of life as role-playing. Rosencrantz and Guildenstern's sincerity was shown to prevent them from embracing the lassez-faire philosophy that life is an old play to be acted according to well-worn rules without regard for its meaning. The cynical attitude of Graham Crowden and the arty contrivance of the choreographed mime sequences by Claude Chagrin brilliantly expressed this 'life-as-a-cheap-entertainment' metaphor. His Le Coq-influenced pantomimes were pretty and arch, the rehearsal of the dumbshow version of *The Mousetrap* from *Hamlet* cleverly condensing in Act II all the action involving Rosencrantz and Guildenstern into a peremptory foreshadowing of their fate. In the players' stylised pantomimes, action became movement, human motivation was reduced to the mechanistic ballet of marionettes.

Hamlet's more dignified notion of the aim of acting (articulated in *Hamlet*, Act III, Scene 2) was undermined by the fact that the Old Vic audience saw the troupe of players on the road to Elsinore touting for trade in a lewd and commercial manner. The Player himself reduced the participation of actors and audience to the level of pornography, archly insinuating that members of the Old Vic audience were, like Rosencrantz and Guildenstern, merely voyeurs.

Another level of acting was introduced into the production five seconds after the exit of the players in Act I. Timed to coincide with the toss of a coin from Rosencrantz to Guildenstern, the scene changed to the interior of the court. Ophelia ran on at this moment in the first of a series of witty dumbshow presentations of speeches or scenes from *Hamlet*.

Stoppard translated Ophelia's narrative description of Hamlet's lunatic behaviour towards her – often used by directors in the past as an excuse for melodramatic stage business by Hamlet – into a series of stage directions which form the basis of a slightly dated pantomime-enactment of the Prince's behaviour as reported in *Hamlet*, Act II, Scene 1 by Ophelia. John McEnery and Caroline John as Hamlet and Ophelia gleefully created a version of the romanticised dumbshow which was typical of second-rate stock productions of the play:

Ophelia runs on in some alarm, holding up her skirts – followed by Hamlet. (Ophelia has been sewing and she holds the garment. They are both mute. Hamlet, with his doublet all unbraced, no hat upon his head, his stockings fouled, ungartered and down-gyved to his ankle, pale as his shirt, his knees knocking each other . . . and with a look so piteous, he takes her by the wrist and holds her hard, then he goes to the length of his arm, and with his other hand over his brow falls to such persual of her face as he would draw it. . . . At last, with a little shaking of his arm, and twice his head waving up and down, he raises a sigh so piteous and profound that it does seem to shatter all his bulk and end his being. That done he lets her go, and with his head over his shoulder turned, he goes out backwards without taking his eyes off her . . . she runs off in the opposite direction.)

(p. 26)

This 'quotation' from stock productions rather than the actual text of *Hamlet* is Stoppard's first, teasing presentation of extracts from the play. In performance it made a prologue to the entrance of Claudius and Gertrude and the first actual words from the Shakespeare text used by Stoppard in conjunction with an old piece of comic business:

> CLAUDIUS: Welcome, dear Rosencrantz ... (*he raises a hand at* GUIL *while* ROS *bows* – GUIL *bows late and hurriedly*) ... and Guildenstern (*he raises a hand at* ROS *while* GUIL *bows to him* ...)
>
> (p. 26)

Wisely, Derek Goldby decided not to guy the scenes from *Hamlet*. Just as the design deliberately commented on the stock scenic elements which have become traditional in staging the play, so were the scenes from *Hamlet* acted in a slightly dated Shakespearean tragic style, nevertheless presenting a sincere reading of the text rather than a burlesque treatment. In contrast to the arch stylisation of the players' mimic performance, the pantomime moments from *Hamlet* were played with the kind of intensity that characterises the most poetic of silent films, challenging the Old Vic audience to 'spot the soliloquy' without the help of the words, while the spoken extracts from the play were staged in a ceremonial style apparently compounded of memories of all the *Hamlet* productions one had ever seen. Through the clever use of clichéd traditions of performance, the quoted extracts from Shakespeare convincingly portended the whole plot of *Hamlet* and were closely enough integrated with the mode of the surrounding action to maintain a subtle tension between 'Shakespeare' and 'Stoppard', continually calling into question the boundaries between Shakespeare's text and its mythic subtext of apocryphal images.

The contrasts in acting style did not disturb the audience's perception of the fictional coherence of the action from one moment to another; the different levels of playing signified different kinds of action in the world of the play, from the intimate, through to the social and political action in the public arena. In fact, the production emphasised the degree

of conscious theatricality which attaches to each mode of
action. A recognisable shape was created as Rosencrantz
and Guildenstern's reactions developed through speech and
movement from the spontaneous and contemporary idiom of
their intimate improvisatory exchanges into a 'double-act'
pattern of question and response followed occasionally by
longer flights of solo speech for more abstract speculation.
The build-up of a dialogue structure reminiscent of the cross-
talk of music hall or variety comedians prepared the audience   for   the   openly   histrionic   rhetorical   displays
(accompanied at times by music and movement) of Graham
Crowden and his troupe.

Having watched Rosencrantz and Guildenstern as audience and critic of the Player and his troupe, the Old Vic
audience was primed to observe and criticise like theatre
professionals the somewhat mechanical interpretation of
Hamlet from a technical point of view. The actors in the
extracts established no rapport with the Old Vic audience.
This action was 'inset' within the performance, its detach-
ment from the audience functioning to enhance the metaphor
of the inexorability of a plot which unfolds according to its
predetermined pattern. Rosencrantz and Guildenstern slip
easily from being an onstage audience to being actors in
Hamlet because their roles are so passive: they merely react
to instructions given and suggestions made by Claudius,
Gertrude and Hamlet. By the time the scenes from *Hamlet*
occurred the production had contrived to suggest, through
a hierarchy of contrasting levels of acting, a theatrical ana-
logue of the relationship between Stoppard's invented
subtext for *Hamlet* and the ritual of an Old Vic *Hamlet*
performance.

Derek Goldby's approach allowed full play to the ironies
inherent in the various meanings of acting – as theatrical
role-playing, conscious social deception, unconscious social
role-playing and spontaneous acts of self-realisation – which
permeate the play. When *Rosencrantz and Guildenstern Are Dead*
is performed with too obvious a break between the style of
Stoppard's prose dialogue and that of Shakespeare's language, then the subtlety of Stoppard's interweaving of
contemporary idiom with Shakespearean rhetoric is lost.

Whenever the play is thus performed as a kind of Shakespeare travesty then the relationship between the audience, Rosencrantz and Guildenstern's world and that of Shakespeare's play disintegrates and the empathy of the audience with the pathos of the two characters is undermined, so that Stoppard's play seems like a repetitious joke at the expense of *Hamlet*. It is true of all Stoppard's major theatrical works that no matter how surprising the complications multiplied on the basis of each play's governing conceit, the jokes are always motivated by their reference to a human experience which elicits empathy from an audience.

The achievement of the Old Vic production was to maintain a delicate balance between the world of Rosencrantz and Guildenstern and Shakespeare's Elsinore, establishing a connection for sophisticated theatregoers between Rosencrantz and Guildenstern's bafflement at the action of Shakespeare's play and their own cynical doubts about the validity of Shakespeare in the contemporary world.

Stride and Petherbridge, through the charm of their performances, engaged the sympathy of the audience for their earnest attempts to know their destiny. At the same time they invited laughter at their failure to do anything more effective than play games in response to the incomprehensible comings and goings which constitute the characters' perspective on *Hamlet*. Although themselves conscious of a difference between their ineffectual stage business (spinning coins, rushing from one end of the stage to the other to find out who was going to come on next, putting up a finger in the wind to determine their geographical location, making silly bets with the players to test the distinction between blind chance and intelligible fate) and the authentic acts of Claudius and Hamlet, they seemed incapable of such authentic action.

Through the close relationship the actors maintained with the audience throughout the performance and the patent sincerity of their performances, they made the audience feel the futility of their stage activity, of the games they were indulging in to escape the omnipresence of death. When each one eventually disappeared into darkness at the end of

the play the production reinforced what Guildenstern had
in Act II implied in his speech to the Player:

> you can't act death. The *fact* of it is nothing to do with seeing
> it happen – it's not gasps and blood and falling about – that
> isn't what makes it death. It's just a man failing to reappear,
> that's all – now you see him, now you don't that's the only
> thing that's real: here one minute and gone the next and
> never coming back – an exit, unobtrusive and unannounced,
> a disappearance gathering weight as it goes on, until, finally,
> it is heavy with death.
>
> (p. 64)

Following their disappearance from the scene in Act III, a
lighting change faded back to the seemingly coherent final
scene from *Hamlet* in which the ambassador of Norway con-
firms the execution of the destiny which has awaited the
protagonists from curtain up.

There is a double irony in the final image of the play
in performance. As Horatio echoed Stoppard's view of the
senselessness of the action of *Hamlet* as pointless melodrama
('so shall you hear of carnal, bloody and unnatural acts, of
accidental judgments, casual slaughters, of deaths put on by
cunning and forced cause, and, in this upshot, purposes
mistook fallen on the inventors' heads'), so was the final
scene itself overwhelmed by darkness and music. Horatio's
speech was itself drowned out by the chaos of sheer theatricality, making Stoppard's (not Shakespeare's) ending rather
sinister. Perhaps, after all, the Player was right. If life is
merely a show, there can be no absolute values, no possibility of faith in anything other than in theatrical performance, in playing the game. 'Audiences know what to expect,
that is all they are prepared to believe in' (p. 64).

If Rosencrantz and Guildenstern's struggle to find the
meaning of their destiny in the ambiguities of *Hamlet* had
failed, members of the Old Vic audience possibly felt the
laughter turning against them as a performance of this
classic humanist drama disintegrated in chaos.

9   THE PROLOGUE IN PERFORMANCE

The play opens in darkness with a voice (which the audience later learns is Archie's) announcing the entrance of Dorothy Moore 'on the occasion of a momentous Radical-Liberal victory at the polls'. This seems like a parody of all the showbiz clichés about the emotionally troubled singing star making a come-back. In the typically unctuous manner of an old-fashioned show business star, Dotty, whom the audience immediately recognises as Diana Rigg in a blonde wig and glittering gold dress, thanks her audience for coming, thanks the pianist as a cue to start and, as the introduction of 'Shine On Harvest Moon' is played, she dries. The musical introduction is repeated. But she still cannot remember her words. When she asks how it begins, offstage voices reply, singing, 'Shine on, shine on harvest moon'. She picks up the words but goes wrong immediately, breaks off after a brief apology typical of such an overwrought show business personality ('No I can't, I'm sorry') and exits to the accompaniment of a drum roll.

At the Old Vic on the evening of 8 February 1972, this is funny for a number of reasons. The performance begins with a performer who is unable to perform, thus immediately disappointing the most basic expectation of any theatre audience at any kind of theatrical performance – the audience is left wondering what possible connection 'Shine on Harvest Moon' could have with a political election. But the laughter is also provoked by the fact that such a hackneyed old cabaret routine is being presented by the National Theatre at the Old Vic and performed by Diana Rigg, known not as a singer or even a serious actress, but as the cool, trendy Emma Peel in the long-running TV detective series, *The Avengers*. Somehow or other various forms of lowbrow entertainment have been conflated in order to create a comic opening to the sophisticated new play the audience has been expecting from their clever young playwright. Surely, none of this is intended to be in earnest? It must be a parody!

Before the audience has time to work out the comic connection between 'Shine On Harvest Moon' and the Radical-
Liberal victory just announced, the 'cries of disappointment'
of the unseen audience off stage, 'change to cries of delight'
as a woman on a trapeze hanging from a chandelier swings
into and out of the spotlight which Dorothy Moore has just
vacated. She is performing a striptease act: every time she
is caught by the spotlight one more article of her clothing
has disappeared. What possible connection can there be
between the falling apart of the singer's routine and this
somewhat eccentric but successfully executed nightclub act?
The spectators' highbrow expectations as members of an
Old Vic audience are being outrageously flouted. To compli-
cate the image, a man in a short white coat, balancing a
tray of drinks on one hand, enters. A waiter? He is unaware
of the striptease taking place behind him; whenever he turns
towards the audience the stripper swings behind him, but
whenever he turns away from the audience in response to
the voices which warn him to get out of the way, there is
nothing for him to see. When the stripper is almost completely naked, the waiter *'backs into the path of the swing and
is knocked arse over tip by a naked lady'*. Again we laugh at the
unexpectedness of seeing such a debased show business routine at the Old Vic theatre, perhaps with the recognition
that we are relieved to find that the play has not started
with a serious philosophical or poetic speech, demanding the
kind of attention which a play by Shakespeare or Samuel
Beckett might. Is our philistine collective unconscious being
stimulated to laugh at the crude slapstick of an innocent
intruder unwittingly becoming a victim in a routine as old
as the clown slipping on a banana skin? Has this waiter
simply strayed into the variety act by mistake? Or is he
knowingly part of the act – a clown with a precisely choreographed routine contrived to enhance the excitement of the
striptease?

As the audience hears the sound of breaking glass in a
blackout, the spotlight moves to illuminate a rather anxious
and irritable man with a lugubrious face who is telephoning
the police to complain about a disturbance of the peace.
The performance now begins to seem reminiscent of a sketch
from an intimate stage revue or a Monty Python gag, in

which one image is yoked incongruously to another to produce random nonsense effects. The first joke which we might
associate with the witty Tom Stoppard occurs during the
telephone conversation when the caller gives his name as
Wittgenstein – possibly the best known and most influential
philosopher of the modern British school. Not only is that
name utterly improbable (we would typically expect him to
say Smith or Jones) but for those who know anything about
Wittgenstein, the lowbrow tone of the performance so far is
placed in a completely different context as the audience is
now introduced to an erudite and facetious level of badinage
which follows in the caller's references to Wagner and 'the
id' in an attempt to spell Wittgenstein. Members of the
audience are alerted to look for in-jokes about modern philosophy – something they would be expecting from the author
of *Rosencrantz and Guildenstern Are Dead*.

A blackout interrupts the conversation after about thirty
seconds. The voice that opened the play announces the
entrance of the 'INCREDIBLE – RADICAL! – LIBERAL!! – JUM-
PERS!!' at which moment eight gymnasts dressed in yellow
tracksuits come tumbling on from different entrances and
converge to form a 'tableau of modest pretension.' They are
followed by Diana Rigg (Dotty) who wanders on in front of
the 'now disassembling tableau'. The circus-like image of a
group of acrobats, interrupted by Diana Rigg who dismisses
them because they are 'still credible', confronts the presumably fearless and, the audience assumes, technically skilled
circus performers with a more human aspect of show business – the cabaret artiste whose professional stock-in-trade
is the exhibition of her emotional vulnerability. The joke is
enhanced by the fact that Diana Rigg's well-known TV
persona in *The Avengers* is cool and efficient, a far cry from
the sentimental and rather dated image of the agonised
chanteuse she is now portraying. The action has something
of the quality of a charade: the audience may wonder
whether her reappearance on stage is intended as a part of
the act or whether it is an interruption of the acrobatic
routine. Indeed it is seldom clear what part of the performance is 'action' and what is merely an aspect of the cabaret
routine. Certain irrelevant figures seem to intrude into the
showbiz routines every now and then, and Dotty keeps switch-

ing from her chanteuse persona to a 'real' personality without warning.

When she calls for 'someone unbelievable', the man who
made the pseudonymous telephone complaint enters as if on
cue, carrying sheets of paper in his hands. Michael Hordern's shambling walk and resigned posture, contrasting
with the expressions of quizzical self-absorption and sup-
pressed outrage that his face so easily assumes, provoke a
huge laugh as he comes onstage seemingly in answer to
Dotty's request for a superb athlete. While the jumpers
continue their somewhat lacklustre acrobatic display, Rigg-
Dotty and Hordern (we now learn that the character's name
is George) resume what appears to be a long-standing marital quarrel. George has just lodged a complaint with the
police against the goings on in what the audience now learns
to be his and Dotty's flat. Dotty unwittingly echoes George's
words as she says, 'I have a complaint. Those people are
supposed to be incredible and I'm not even astonished. I'm
not even faintly surprised', a line which gets a big laugh as
members of the audience concur that the performance they
have witnessed, though startlingly unexpected on the stage
of the Old Vic, is hardly impressive as a genuine circus
act. According to Dotty she sings better than they jump
and 'can probably jump higher than they can sing'.
(Another laugh here as Diana Rigg is not known to be a
singer.)

The first explanation of the meaning of this odd cocktail
of performance events comes when Dotty turns on George
furiously, 'It's my bloody party, George'. As George exits she
makes preparations to perform her song again, commenting
caustically all the while on the inadequacy of the acrobatic
turn. When she tells her pianist that she intends to 'do the
one about the moon' she reveals a sophisticated perception
of the clichés of her own performance. Again, however, she
cannot even manage to remember the clichés but can only
drift randomly from one evergreen moon ballad to the other
until she manages, 'fortuitously', to sing six words of 'Blue
Moon' in the correct order. Stoppard, having deconstructed
the typical act of the chanteuse (just as Dorothy has sarcasti-
cally deconstructed the jumpers' routine) now permits the

Old Vic audience a momentary glimpse of the act as it should be.

Now gaining confidence, she starts to play the chanteuse, strolling in and out among the dogged jumpers, moving upstage of them and turning. Quite a few critics commented on the effectiveness of Diana Rigg's singing, a fact which suggests that part of the pleasure of the performance was derived from seeing a well-known actress demonstrating unexpected skills. As Dorothy sings a conflation of 'Moon-glow' and 'Blue Moon' the jumpers assemble themselves into a human pyramid which hides her from the view of the audience. From this point, it is apparent that Dotty is not drunk, as some members of the audience may have suspected, but is in the throes of a mental breakdown. The tawdry show business context has a further connotation, some kind of sexual liaison between Dotty and the jumpers being implied by her jeering words, 'Jumpers, I've had – yellow, I've had them all. Incredible, *barely* credible, credible and all too bloody likely – when I say jump, *jump!*' (p.12). Here it should be observed that Diana Rigg's beauty and glamour were emphasised in almost every newspaper review, so it is not fanciful to suggest that connotations of sexual misconduct were given a prominence in the performance which they may not appear to have on the page.

A gunshot is heard, a jumper is blown out of the pyramid and the music stops. Did Dotty fire the shot? That would explain her last command. She walks through the gap left by the shot jumper and he pulls himself up against her legs, dying. She calls for Archie as she holds the jumper under his arms, in shock. Now the pyramid, 'slowly collapses into the dark, imploding on the missing part'. As Dotty remains frozen in the spotlight, the party sounds return, slightly more high-pitched than at the opening of the play. In response to Archie's announcement that 'the party is over' a drunken voice sings offstage, 'It's time to call it a day', thus completing the opening chorus of a well-known ballad appropriate to the repertoire of a chanteuse such as Dotty. Ironically now, after all the facetiousness of the preceding high-jinks, the joke and the applause and cheers of the responsive party-goers, although they literally complete the charade of

'name the tune' in slick show business fashion, begin to seem
grotesquely inappropriate as the party noise fades while
Dotty is left with the dead jumper in an eerie frozen moment
during which a trendy white bedroom – hers presumably –
assembles around her. As if in response to her earlier call,
Archie appears and the ensuing dialogue reveals that the
dead man is Duncan McFee. In trying to help Dotty keep
the death in proportion, Archie says, 'Death is always a
great pity of course but it's not as though the alternative
were immortality'. The cynicism of this statement provokes
a laugh because it is spoken by Archie (Graham Crowden)
in deadly earnest – another example of the disjunction
between the reality of the events being presented and the
glossy showbiz format of presentation.

Now the spotlight, which has been the one constant factor
within the almost surreal succession of images, is focused on
the giant TV screen at the back of the bedroom to become
a map of the pitted surface of the moon as photographed
by satellite: this gives way to a close-up of the moon which
is then lost as members of the audience perceive that they
are watching a TV programme about something happening
on the moon. The TV image changes to reveal various
different views of a moon-landing, while the general lighting
now on in the bedroom reveals Dotty still in the same
position, holding up the corpse of a gymnast in yellow track-
suit trousers and singlet.

At this point George is simultaneously in view, working
at the desk in his study – a clever theatrical exploitation of
the stock cinematic technique of widening from close-up
(the moon) to a wide-angle shot with Dotty's bedroom and
George's study revealed in full. Up to now, only a very small
part of the stage space has been visible in the spotlight,
although the image within it has changed from one moment
to the next. Most of the stage has been in darkness, but as
the spotlight transforms into an image of the moon on a
TV screen showing a programme about a moon-landing the
audience is made to question the status of all the preceding
images. Has this all been a representation of twelve minutes
of television-viewing, complete with the usual switching from
one channel to another? The montage of images might easily

have given a spectator that impression. And the presence of Diana Rigg may lead some of the Old Vic audience to connect this montage with the clever title sequence of *The Avengers*. But if so, what is Diana Rigg doing in a 'real' bedroom with a TV news programme on in the background? Where are the boundaries between life and theatre, theatre and TV image, TV image and reality?

The contrast between George, calmly at work on one side of the stage, and Dotty, supporting a corpse on the other, is grotesquely funny. This absurd contrast is heightened by the entrance of the waiter/butler figure from the striptease sequence, through what seems to be the front door. He is now dressed in the grey overall of a janitor and is singing another ballad reminiscent of those we have heard previously, 'Gonna make a sentimental journey'. Is this still part of the extended cabaret performance of which Dotty's turn was intended to be the highlight? When Dotty asks if it's Archie, the man identifies himself as Crouch before exiting through another door, after which Dotty sinks on to the bed with the corpse slumped over her knees. By now this rather poignant image has become comic as the audience watches the bemused Dotty wondering what she is going to do to get rid of the corpse. Gradually, the prologue begins to emerge as distinct from the action of the play which is beginning in earnest, although the audience is still being repeatedly ambushed as Stoppard plays a series of theatrical games designed to undermine its certainty about the proper method of interpreting the theatrical signs with which it is being presented.

Dotty is incapable of doing anything other than watch television at present, for she turns up the volume to allow the audience to hear what constitutes an explanation by a newsreader of the images it has just been viewing on the large screen behind her bed. Apparently the astronaut is Captain Scott, the first Englishman to set foot on the moon. He is returning to earth, having left behind him second-in-command Astronaut Oates, who is seen 'waving forlornly' from the featureless wastes of the lunar landscape. At last one feels the moon songs might be leading somewhere! Somehow the play is going to turn out to be about man's conquest of the moon.

But the news broadcast is surely an ironic reminder of Scott and Oates at the Antarctic some seventy years before. The first Oates had heroically chosen to sacrifice his life in the hope of saving the life of his fellow-explorer, Captain Scott; this Oates is being deserted by his superior officer. Before one has time to puzzle out this conundrum, Dotty has changed the channel and one is watching with her what appears to be a military celebration in the centre of London. Five seconds of this give way to a three-second snippet of a commercial until Dotty flips channels to catch the moon programme again. The announcer is now explaining how Captain Scott prevented Astronaut Oates from re-entering the space capsule by knocking him off the ladder to its entrance, thus ensuring that he himself would survive the return journey in a damaged space craft.

This piece of information is immediately succeeded by the military procession as Dotty switches channels again. Against a background of military music, Dotty takes off her bloodstained dress as Crouch enters with a bin of rubbish and several empty champagne bottles, the first proper clue that the surreal stream of images represents the late-night high jinks of a celebration party. After informing Dotty that it is nine o'clock, Crouch leaves by what is obviously the front door of an apartment, passing George's secretary on her way to his study. Crouch apparently fails to notice her as she takes off her overcoat and hat but the absurd thing about this otherwise mundane moment is that it involves a repeat on a commonplace domestic level of the circus-type striptease incident the audience has witnessed earlier, in which Crouch – for we have now learnt who he is – kept brushing past the stripper unaware of her existence. Those in the audience with keen eyesight will recognise the secretary as the stripper. Just as she is now rather more modestly taking off some items of clothing so does he repeat the action of brushing past her in the style of a waiter with bottles in hand. It is an incredible coincidence, yet quite plausible in the context of colliding images one has been witnessing since the show began.

The audience laughs at the perception that when something incredible finally does happen, as if in answer to
Dotty's earlier demand, it takes place in an atmosphere of
serene calm. The secretary's straitlaced composure as she
enters the study and sits with pen poised waiting to take
dictation from George forms a bizarre contrast with her
exhibitionistic performance the previous evening. One laughs
because the actors' attitudes suggest that such wild parties
occur so routinely at this address that they may be regarded
with bored nonchalance by the most conventional of people.

The recurring shifts from one strange action or image to
another are now succeeded by the static tableau of an
absent-minded middle-aged don about to give dictation to
a po-faced secretary. The image's frozen serenity is disturbed
only slightly by the intrusion of Dotty's quiet cries for help
to which the audience may feel George is about to respond,
but his movement of the head has apparently been merely
a pause for thought and he continues to write, as the bedroom in which Dotty stands propping up the corpse of one
Duncan McFee is blacked out.

George now gets up to dictate to his secretary from the
notes he has written. What will he say? Is *this* a rationalis-
ation of the very confusing series of images/events the audience has just witnessed? Given the build-up of one's
expectations, his first word – 'secondly' – is very funny,
immediately exposing the absent-mindedness of one who
cannot remember on which sheet of paper he wrote the
opening of the lecture but also deflating the portentousness
of this moment of intensely anticipated revelation. Michael
Hordern is a master of this kind of comic playing, in which
every flicker across his face registers, with the intensity of a
great clown, the eternal surprise of a man as consistently
ambushed by his own intellectual ingenuity as he is regularly
tripped up by the banal physical obstacles he fails to notice
around him.

While actually giving the audience all the basic exposition
of the play, Stoppard has apparently denied it any information about the meaning or status of the images or events
it has witnessed. Now, just as most members of the audience
feel they are on safe ground, George begins in the middle

of his speech! What one has in fact been witnessing on stage are events within a context which cannot be satisfactorily explained, a joke which re-enacts one of the primary themes of George's argument – that it is impossible to determine the point of origin of the world because one would have to go back to an infinite fraction to establish that first moment of existence after nothingness and since one can never (except in logic) actually reach infinity, one can never actually perceive or experience the beginning. One begins in the middle.

But George does find the right note and for the sake of rhetoric starts, 'To begin at the beginning', this time only to be interrupted by Dotty's panic stricken cries, 'Help! Murder!' (p.15). George responds in fury by throwing his notes on the desk and moving towards the door. Again, the audience is led to expect a big confrontation scene between Dotty and George in which he might discover her with the dead gymnast and, one might assume, help her do something about getting rid of the body. Before he reaches the door, we hear her shouting out what we recognise as Macduff's words on discovering the corpse of Duncan in Act II, Scene 3 of *Macbeth* ('Oh horror, horror, horror. . . . Confusion now hath made his masterpiece. Most sacrilegious murder'), appropriate under the circumstances for the Old Vic audience has already learned that the dead jumper's name was Duncan. While George pauses with his hand on the door handle, members of the audience may wonder if this is all part of a sophisticated game of charades. Diana Rigg uses a different voice to distinguish Lady Macbeth's voice from Macduff's. Can Dotty be in *real* distress and behave so playfully? Perhaps George realises it is a game. This would explain why he ignores her screams and returns to his work: 'To begin at the beginning: Is God?' (p.15).

In the context of the lowbrow entertainment which the audience has so far witnessed, the portentousness of this large question and Hordern's comic inability to relate to the actuality of the surrounding context is hilarious. By the end of *Jumpers* the audience will understand the relationship between the extended showbiz montage and the question 'Is God?' But at this point the question strikes one as the most outrageous non sequitur in the history of theatre. Time and time again during the first twelve minutes of *Jumpers*, Stoppard has brilliantly succeeded in ambushing his Old Vic audience. And by the end of the play, the repeated interruptions, anti-climaxes and shifts of focus from image to seemingly unrelated image, will have created a pattern of audience response which echoes the recurring experience of the central characters, bewildered by their confrontation with a universe the evidence of whose reality tends to disintegrate or disappear whenever they attempt to grasp it – for either pragmatic or analytical purposes.

This opposition of show business and philosophy underlies the structure of the whole play, reflecting a genuine uncertainty about whether human behaviour ought properly to be judged by standards of pragmatic efficiency or of logical consistency and coherence. In the play, the same action is repeated from the perspective represented by each of the foregoing attitudes. The audience of the Old Vic is ingeniously prepared for the ensuing dialectic between philosophical argument and slapstick action. More and more complex frames of interpretation are successively offered to encapsulate the initial stream of sensory images. The data given in the television-style montage (representing the way one confronts the contemporary world) become intelligible from various competing perspectives for the rest of the evening. The challenge for the audience is to choose an interpretation which does justice to the complexity and detail of this flood of sensory information

10 VISUAL ASPECTS OF PRODUCTION

The opening sequences of images established the theatrical game that Stoppard would be playing with the Old Vic audience for the rest of the evening. By the time George had dictated the first two minutes of his lecture members of the audience had begun to understand how spectacle and philosophical debate were connected. Stoppard at this moment consolidated his reputation for combining the razzle-dazzle of show-business with flights of virtuoso word play that transformed the twists and turns of complex intellectual arguments into high comedy.

Peter Wood, who has directed all the London productions of Stoppard's major full-length plays for the theatre since *Jumpers*, cleverly integrated the various aspects of the play to achieve a style of comic performance which became a model for subsequent productions of Stoppard's stage plays. From an actor's and director's point of view, the major difficulty of the play is how to sustain an audience's concentration on the complex philosophical argument of George's lecture while simultaneously maintaining the momentum of the farcical whodunnit which has been introduced in the opening *coup de theâtre*.

Once the dizzying succession of show business images slowed down, the Old Vic audience saw Dotty at stage right standing in a white bedroom holding the corpse of Duncan McFee. The futuristic, high-tech bedroom had a door to the hallway (formed by a narrow strip of stage at centre) adjoining George's study which was just visible on the extreme stage left-hand side of the proscenium opening. Patrick Robertson's set was mounted on a revolve which it was possible to position so that sections of the bedroom, hallway and study were simultaneously visible to the audience. After the first surreptitious scene change from the neutral black background of the prologue to the white bedroom, the revolve literally moved to the centre of the stage first George's study then Dotty's bedroom. This movement of the stage in full view of the audience dramatised the shift from the abstract level of conceptual problems to the mundane level of domestic and personal difficulties which gave a startling immediacy to George's ethical speculations.

The sequence of scenes being revolved into place was as follows: prologue; bedroom; study; bedroom; hall; study; bedroom; study; bedroom; study; hall; bedroom; coda (the same position on the revolve as the prologue). This pattern reinforced the sense of competing perspectives created by the prologue. The scenes taking place in the bedroom presented the failure of Dotty and George's marriage, probably the real cause of the mental breakdown which she attributes to the 'rape' of the moon. Naturally, the scenes in the study were chiefly concerned with George's dictation of his paper. Dotty never entered the study although her cries often interrupted George's composition of the paper. The hallway was a neutral space from which Bones launched his criminal investigations and where confidences were exchanged by Bones, Archie and Crouch, concerning the murder of McFee. The frenetic opening and closing of doors in traditional farce was evoked in the rapid succession of entrances and exits of the secretary, Crouch, Archie, Bones and George himself at various moments.

Patrick Robertson used the fashionable decor of a Mayfair apartment to connect the show business imagery of the prologue with the trendy milieu in which the action of the play occurs. The immediate visual impression was of shiny white, horizontal lines which curved to frame bookshelves, the cupboard in the bedroom and the large TV screen behind Dotty's bed with its white, shaggy bedcover – in fact, a series of screens. At the stage right of the bedroom there was a door to the bathroom adjacent to French windows supposedly leading on to a balcony. The futuristic effect of the decor conveyed an impression of space age modernity, making a deliberate comment on a world in which media technology had triumphed over humane values. A large Snoopy toy on the bed stood out against the sleek impersonality of the decor, nicely echoing the way George's stooped posture and ruffled clothes and manner set him apart from the chic consumerism reflected in the surrounding environment. Significantly, one of the reviewers commented on the fact that George's old desk was the only item on the set which did not match the monochrome trendiness of the decor.

The overall motif, of white frames surrounding grey screens against a black background, reinforced the impact of the white spotlight against the surrounding darkness in the prologue sequence, echoing the image of the moon in the darkness of space which was repeated again in the white semi-spherical glass side-lamps and in the glass fish bowl

which Dotty placed over her head in the charade of the
Moon and Sixpence. This monochromatic decor was contrasted with the yellow (proverbially the colour of the moon
but also signifying cowardice and duplicity) of the jumpers'
tracksuits, the gold lurex of Dotty's figure-hugging showbiz
outfit and the yellow and gold colours of the ecclesiastical
garments worn in the coda.

Graham Crowden's Archie reminded one of a 1920s
dandy, in a black mohair suit with yellow lining and with
black bow tie, an orchid, an opera cape, yellow handkerchief,
wide-brimmed black hat and smoking a cigarette in a very
long cigarette holder. Unlike George, Archie's clothes perfectly matched the slick 'designer' milieu which is the visual
emblem of the Rad-Lib ethos. George was dressed in a cross
between the traditional tweed suit of the university don, and
the mod Carnaby Street gear of the late 1960s with loose
brown cavalry twill trousers, a greeny-brown woollen cardi-
gan, brown shoes, a patterned silk scarf and a lightly patterned white, green and purple shirt of the sort which was
popular among bohemian types who might identify with the
'love-and-peace' values of the hippies without going the
whole way. The secretary (Anna Carteret) wore a white
'wet-look' overcoat, a matching mid-calf length skirt and
white blouse. For her domestic scenes, Diana Rigg wore a
white chiffon gown over a white negligee with feather trim-
ming. Bones (David Ryall) was dressed conventionally in a
three-piece tweed suit and a fawn raincoat with his pink
carnation a give-away sign of his secret passion for musical
comedy. Dotty, Archie, the secretary and the jumpers were
associated through colour with the glamorous showbiz milieu
whereas George, Bones and Crouch visually stood out
against it.

Stoppard's ingenious use of props is difficult to comprehend fully unless the play is seen in performance. A running
gag was set up when George attempted to demonstrate
Zeno's notion of infinite series ('since an arrow shot towards
a target first had to cover half the distance, and then half
the remainder and then half the remainder after that, and
so on *ad infinitum*, the result was, as I will now demonstrate,
that though an arrow is always approaching its target, it

never quite gets there, and Saint Sebastian died of fright',
p.19). George's somewhat eccentric methods of illustrating
his arguments provided not merely uproariously funny
moments within the performance, they also motivated his
own subsequent absent-minded progress through the plot.
For it was his own accidental shooting of the arrow in
startled response to Dotty's attention-seeking cry of 'fire'
which, unbeknownst to him at the time, caused the death
of his pet hare Thumper and therefore left him for the rest
of the play searching for Thumper in order to resume the
visual demonstration by way of the tortoise and hare par-
able. The motivation for extending the visual aspects of the
prologue into the succeeding action of the play thus derived
from George's bizarre illustrations of the palpable difference
between the logically possible and coherent world of the
philosopher and the actual world.

In his meanderings across the stage in search of Thumper,
George was brought for the first time since the prologue into
contact with Dotty whose '*nude body* [he discovers] *sprawled
face down, and apparently lifeless on the bed*'. There was a huge
laugh on Michael Hordern's deadpan 'take' as he ignored
her and went to the bathroom to find Thumper. This was
another instance of Stoppard's effective exploitation of a
visual tableau to evoke the characters' attitudes and relationships. (One would have to be blind not to respond to such
a beautiful body, yet George was interested only in his
philosophy demonstration!) Typically, Stoppard followed the
visual gag with a playful explanation of its logical significance:

GEORGE: Are you a proverb?
DOTTY: No, I'm a book.
GEORGE: *The Naked and the Dead*
DOTTY: Stay with me! . . .
    Play with me . . .
GEORGE: (*Hesitating*) Now . . . ?
DOTTY: I mean *games* – (p.21)

This short exchange not only established the motif of game-
playing, in this case charades, which were the equivalent for
Dotty of George's live philosophy demonstrations, but it also

encapsulated with great economy the state of their relationship.

By drawing a parallel between George's struggle to express
his philosophical argument in visual terms and Dotty's
attempt to communicate her desperation in the form of a
charade, the play in performance implied the possibility of
rationally explaining all the bizarre visual gags which had
so far been witnessed. The production seemed teasingly to
offer further clues for the interpretation of the accumulating
action of *Jumpers* on both the logical and psychological levels.
As the action progressed, the clues multiplied and the solution to the mystery seemed more and more unattainable.
At the end, the performance left one feeling that although
one had grasped the significance of individual moments of
action or theatrical spectacle, the overwhelming confusion of
the high-tech, media-saturated milieu might represent a
human fall from grace. The impossibility of perceiving or
experiencing the world in a pristine state had been demonstrated in utterly theatrical terms by the rococo elaboration
of one visual joke upon another. As a member of the audience, one had shared in the process of growth towards an
adult recognition of the paradox that the passionate quest
for truth in the modern world has led to the dissolution of
certainties.

While a reading of the play makes one most aware of the
ethical dilemma connected with the murder of McFee, a
performance invites one to experience the problems of perception which underline this ethical dilemma. By surrounding the action with the monochromatic frames of the moving
set, Peter Wood's production provoked a subliminal awareness of competing perceptual perspectives, of the way in
which one's angle of vision alters the appearance of what is
being viewed.

11   ACTING AND CHARACTERISATION

Reading reviews of the 1972 Old Vic production of *Jumpers*,
one is struck by the way in which the personality and skill
of the two leading actors were regarded as contributing as
much to the success of the performance as the originality
and wit of the text. Every reviewer regarded the astonishing
performance of Michael Hordern as one of the major reasons
for the success of the performance. But, interestingly, some
critics referred to Diana Rigg's 'moon' speech as the high
point of the evening while other reviews read like fan letters
in praise of her beauty and charm. These responses reveal-
ingly suggest a major difference between a play on the page
and a play on the stage. The point has been made in Part
One of this book that the text of the play makes full sense
only if George and Dotty's situation is both funny and
moving, if members of the audience are able to identify with
the characters' alienation from the cynical materialism of
the society they inhabit as well as to laugh at it. Like
Rosencrantz and Guildenstern, they are essentially innocents
in a corrupt world where the majority have learned to play
the game. (Significantly, Graham Crowden, who had been
so effective as the Player in *Rosencrantz and Guildenstern Are
Dead*, was cast as the arch-relativist Archie).

Jumpers is a more complex and elaborate play than *Rosencrantz and Guildenstern Are Dead* and the action, although wittily contrived, is at the same time more or less naturalist-
ically motivated. Everything that occurs could be accounted
for in terms of a 'naturalistic' TV thriller like *The Avengers*.
At the same time, the improbable nature of the joke-like
stage action is flaunted by Stoppard. If the performance is
not merely to suggest a virtuoso surrealist farce (such as
Stoppard's earlier *After Magritte*) its astonishing verbal and
visual conceits must be grounded in the passionate nature
of the actors' humanity. It is likely that Rigg and Hordern
in 1972 came closest of all the actors who have essayed these
roles to achieving the perfect balance between sympathy for
the pathos of the characters' failure to realise their ideals,

and comic poise in portraying the absurdity of the way they behave in the attempt.

Neither Hordern nor Rigg made any Stanislavskian attempt to *become* their characters in performance, yet each obviously felt a degree of empathy with the character's situation. Their characterisations were in the style of a sophisticated comedy of upper class manners as exemplified by Noel Coward's classic comedies, *Hay Fever* or *Private Lives*. While a definite realism was maintained in the presentation of their relationship, the quality of self-consciousness which they demonstrated in manipulating their own stage personalities ensured that the verbal arabesques of George's lecture and the sophisticated self-awareness inherent in Dotty's own disillusionment did not contradict a more spontaneous presentation of feeling at other moments in their performances. The casting allowed Diana Rigg to exploit the glamour of her television persona to the full. This contrasted perfectly with Hordern's superb use of the battered face which he had previously employed to great effect on stage or film in the portrayal of demented idealists, eccentric wits or shrewd old men.

The unequal relationship of husband and wife in terms of age and physique was reflected in the reviewers' often lengthy descriptions of the physical features of the two central characterisations, another aspect of the play which would not strike a reader as significant: 'Michael Hordern, those woe-begone, bloodhound features massively working overtime, wrestles marvellously with the complex syntax and moral anguish of the philosopher: Diana Rigg, sumptuous in a fur-lined gown, sails glamorously through the part of the showbiz wife' (Michael Billington in the *Guardian*, 3 February 1972).

It is interesting that Billington describes both performances in terms of movement, indicating something of the way in which each actor expressed the inner state of the character through a repertoire of typical facial expressions and body movements, George doggedly in pursuit of his logical solution, Dotty (as her name implies) vaguely going through the motions of the chanteuse's display of emotions, while in fact moving aimlessly about her room as though drifting on the sea of her uncertainties. A few reviewers precisely described both the quality of Hordern's walk and the way in which he enacted the movement of his thoughts.

> Walking an invisible line and stuffing his pockets down almost to his knees in his cardigan, Michael Hordern picks up the memory of Jonathan Miller's A. J. Ayer parody in *Beyond the Fringe* and projects it on a sublime scale; pouring out endless strings of subtle parentheses with desperate speed lest the lines of thought escape him.
>
> (Irving Wardle, *The Times*, 3 February, 1972)

Stoppard's witty harnessing of high ideas and low comedy was praised by Harold Hobson, who commented in *The Sunday Times* on the way in which the discipline of academic philosophy was combined with the virtues of Brian Rix and *La Plume de ma Tante* (a 1950s revue from which Stoppard borrowed the gag of Dotty's cupboard door opening whenever the bedroom door closed). In extolling both the wit and physical beauty of Diana Rigg's performance (a number of reviews mention that she appeared naked at various points in the play) and the comic intensity which Hordern gave George's pursuit of a proof for the existence of God, the critics were responding to the way in which Stoppard and Peter Wood had managed to illustrate vividly the tension between flesh and spirit which *Jumpers* reveals as central to modern life. Hobson's review is quite specific about Hordern's illumination of this dialectic:

> Michael Hordern plays the professor with a passionate intellectual devotion, a comic variety, an ability to move instantly from mental certainty to physical bewilderment.
>
> (*Sunday Times*, 6 February 1972)

The flatness of the other type characters was also noticed by the reviewers, as was the skill of Graham Crowden (Archie), David Ryall (Bones), Paul Curran (Crouch) and Anna Carteret (Secretary) in mimicking with economy the particular acting style usually associated with each particular stage type. The eccentric humanity of each figure was apprehended, not through three-dimensional details of characterisation but in the contradictions between the mask of personality and the oddly inappropriate private interests of each. The contradiction between private self and professional persona was entirely consistent with the odd attraction which Dotty and George feel towards each other.

A more detailed analysis of the performance would include a description of the actors' brilliant timing of the verbal wit and the succession of bizarre and often unashamedly plagiarised visual gags, but this would involve much repetition of points already made. It will perhaps suffice to remark on the unexpected poignancy which Diana Rigg instilled in Dotty's speeches on the violation of the moon and the depth of emotion evinced by Michael Hordern as George discovered the dead hare Thumper and accidentally killed the tortoise Pat. Obliquely, these moments signified both the idealism and the failure represented by the marriage of Dotty and George. Such complex interaction of comedy and feeling could only have been evoked by artists of the calibre of Mr Hordern and Miss Rigg.

The Real Thing – Strand Theatre, 1982

12   PLAYING WITH WEST END CONVENTIONS

In response to Rosencrantz's question in *Rosencrantz and Guildenstern Are Dead*, 'Shouldn't we be doing something constructive?' Guildenstern says, 'What did you have in mind? A short blunt human pyramid?' In an interview with Ronald Hayman (1977), Stoppard admitted that this image was the starting point for *Jumpers*: 'I thought: 'How marvellous to have a pyramid of people on a stage, and a rifle shot and one member of the pyramid just being blown out of it and the others imploding on the hole as he leaves.' I really like theatrical events . . .' (Ronald Hayman, *Tom Stoppard*, London, 1979).

Stoppard has often used earlier plays as starting points for later ones. Elements of the radio play, *Artist Descending a*

Staircase (1972), were brilliantly transformed into the bravura stage play, *Travesties* (1974); the comic radio play about spies, *The Dog it Was That Died* (1982), was used as a jumping-off point for the much more complex stage play, *Hapgood* (1988); and he himself said in an interview in 1981 that '*Professional Foul* and *Jumpers* can each be described as a play about a moral philosopher preoccupied with the true nature of absolute morality, trying to separate absolute values from local ones and local situations' (*Gambit*, No. 37, 1981).

In *The Real Thing* the title of Henry's play *The House of Cards* lends emblematic significance to the 'pyramidical, tiered viaduct' which the architect is erecting at the moment in Scene 1 when his wife slams the door, causing the pyramid of playing cards to collapse. While the image itself is rather contrived (a fact to which the title of Henry's play draws attention) it is conceived on a very different scale from the ostentatious acrobatic trick which goes awry in *Jumpers*, although here again, it is used in jest at the beginning of the play to signify the collapse of an ordered world of human relationships and its replacement by the uncertainty which characterises the adult perception of contemporary life. One is immediately struck by the way Stoppard has 'domesticated' the circus-style acrobatics of *Jumpers*, accommodating the image to a wholly naturalistic stage environment.

Where in *Jumpers* the image was employed as part of the overall motif of show business performance, in the later play it introduces the idea of architecture which is prevalent throughout. The architect in the play-within-the-play, *House of Cards*, parallels the figure of the playwright in the play proper. An architect constructs the order in which people live their lives; he designs the settings for the stages on which relationships are played out. In *The Real Thing* architecture and interior design become metaphors for the way in which people choose to conduct their personal relationships. The complex scenic parallels constructed by Stoppard in conjunction with Peter Wood, the director of the first production, and their designer, Carl Toms, make visible the relation between human behaviour and the rooms which create its environment.

In the theatre, an audience engages with the action first

as theatrical event, and only later as narrative. While it is true that in the performance *The Real Thing* did not possess the obvious surface theatricality of *Jumpers* or *Rosencrantz and Guildenstern Are Dead*, reviews of the London production (1982), in describing the structure of the play and its philosophical arguments repeatedly mentioned specific visual and musical effects. Stage props and settings were fastidiously chosen to enable the audience to grasp the outline of the argument while adhering to naturalistic conventions for the presentation of situation and action. *Jumpers* had teased audiences with emblematic images of gymnastics, musical comedy routines, George's bow and arrow, the hare and the tortoise and continual references to the moon, images which reminded one throughout the evening that the dramatic structure took its form from the opposition between a philosophy lecture and a cabaret routine, both extremely self-conscious forms of performance. Performance of *The Real Thing* subtly persuaded audiences that the action was taking place in the day-to-day world of bourgeois social reality: even when the play did employ specific props as illustrations of its arguments, Stoppard had carefully contrived a naturalistic justification for the presence of each object in its place on the set.

13 VISUAL ASPECTS: SET AND PROPS

Carl Toms' set created a series of pictorial framing devices at the same time as it evoked the peculiarly bland neutrality of interior decoration which characterised the 'designer' milieu of the affluent middle classes in the early 1980s. There were no walls surrounding the furniture for each indoor location, only grey gauze panels which indicated where walls might be but which were themselves translucent: 'Seven panels face out front, rising simply, sometimes in threes or fours to frame the action' (Michael Coveney, *Financial Times*). Like the action of the play itself, the scenery more or less denoted real locations but was at the same time abstract enough to seem entirely emblematic whenever appropriate. Most striking was the way in which the screens were arranged to create different appertures for viewing the action at the beginnings and ends of scenes before they were flown out as a scene proper began. This had the effect of framing each scene so that the 'life' which the actors were portraying was at the same time perceived by the audience as though it were a work of art.

This self-referential effect was continued in the parallels established between artefacts within the scene and the action of the play itself as artefact constructed for the entertainment of the spectator. The key to this baroque game of self-referencing which provided a philosophical framework for the play's presentation of experience is supplied in the opening of *House of Cards*-play-within-*The Real Thing*. The deliberately contrived effect of using a small piece of stage business (the collapse of the playing cards) to signify the break-up of the relationship between the architect and his wife as a result of his discovery of her infidelity, drew attention to the theme of architecture as design for living. Because of its positioning within a play-within-the-play it reminded the audience moreover of the potentially symbolic function of naturalistic stage business and of the contrivance of the Noel Coward-like pattern of action and witty dialogue in *House of Cards*, with its ironic similarities to the more messy and complicated (yet nonetheless evidently contrived) action and dialogue of Scene 2 – the first 'real' action of *The Real Thing*.

Having established the principle that the overtly symbolic significance of a stage prop in a well-made play is no less contrived than the most colloquial dialogue and complex situation in a naturalistic play, the production proceeded freely to exploit the idea that the most banal, flat surfaces of modern life as reproduced in photography become works of art when distinguished by a particular quality of self-awareness. Hanging behind the sofa in Henry and Charlotte's living room (Scene 2) was a painting of Henry and Charlotte on their classic English sofa. The painting bore a deliberate resemblance to David Hockney's famous painting of himself and his friend Celia. Apart from the obvious self-referential quality of the painting, which provoked a kind of 'Chinese boxes' meditation on levels of representation (the painting, the stage scenery and the real environment which the set portended) Carl Toms' clever extension of Stoppard's technique of multiple self-reflection made an initial parallel with the architect's house of playing cards (Scene 1) and its emblematic reverberations.

By now, members of the audience had grasped an essential feature of the scenic design which looked flat and minimalist in the style of a Hockney painting of the 1970s. Like many of Hockney's portraits of people in their homes, the set framed characters in a visual field which appeared to reveal as a set of structural relations the connections among a group of trendy people analogous with the grouping of items of decor that signified the chic minimalist principles of contemporary environments designed or chosen by their inhabitants. In visual terms, the scenery promoted a dialectic between the beauty of simplicity and its banality, at the same time echoing the confrontation of genuine passion with emotional emptiness or cliché experienced by the main characters. Apart from changes in the disposition of the furniture, the actual scenic background appeared to vary very little.

Furniture for individual scenes was set on a series of movable sections of the stage (trucks) which could slide either from back to front or from one side of the stage to the other, allowing furniture to be 'trucked' smoothly on to the centre of the stage without holding up the action but reminding the audience of the mechanics of theatre production which effect the scenic transitions from one location to another. The grey gauze panels indicated walls without representing them; doors which one supposed led to other rooms were present mostly at upstage left and right. There was a different design approach to the interior of the train compartment (Scenes 6 and 11) which, because it consisted virtually of a two-dimensional stage flat behind two leather-upholstered bench seats, gave the impression of being a 'cut-out' set in a TV studio.

During each scene change, the screens in the proscenium opening descended to allow for a slide projection. At the

end of *The House of Cards* scene the architect shook the toy
which his wife had given him as a souvenir, thus creating
an Alpine snowstorm in a glass bowl. The fake quality of
the souvenir made a witty counterpoint to the architect's
genuine experience of dislocation as his comfortable world
fell apart – signified by the projection of the glass bowl
snowstorm (hugely enlarged, of course) on to the front
screens so as to 'engulf the stage'. This final image of *The
House of Cards* play functioned as a gimmick to cover the
scene change to Scene 2 but it also implied that the Alpine
toy was on a number of levels a fake – as a souvenir (for
the wife had not in fact gone to Switzerland but had bought
the souvenir to make her pretence credible), as an alibi (for
it turned out that she did not have a lover so that there was
no real need for the pretence), and as a typically commercial
modern artefact which debased the beautiful image of a real
place to the level of a tourist cliché.

A corresponding image of the cliché value of a tourist
souvenir being used as an alibi occurs at the end of Scene
9. The slide projection of tartan fabric echoes Annie's gift
of a tartan fabric scarf to Henry as a souvenir of her visit
to Glasgow during which she has probably slept with her
fellow actor, Billy. The discourse on the authenticity of the
socially constructed perception of the contemporary environment was extended in the slide projections designed by Carl
Toms to accompany every scene change. Views of streets
in fashionable London residential areas such as Islington
alternated with slides of the Hammersmith Bridge and a
large crane, suggesting that even the landscape of the city
is today a type of designer environment which generations
of architects destroy and remake as a kind of stage setting
for urban living. Interestingly, the radio programme *Desert
Island Discs*, on which Henry appears as a guest, evoked
an image of a wholly natural environment, a space wholly
untransformed by culture. Yet Henry finds it difficult to
choose suitable music to take to the island, his taste being
too lowbrow to be appropriate for a sophisticated playwright.
The 'off stage' existence of this culturally undetermined and
imaginary place (as a space for nostalgic fantasies of pre-
cultural existence) is once paralleled on stage in the empty

space of Scene 8. Here theatre itself became the most complete metaphor for the paradoxical nature of acting as both being and pretending.

The empty space is a potent image of the real space of theatre, transformed by the pretence of actors into the imaginary places of a drama. It is at once here and nowhere, this space and some other place, localised and general, real space and imaginary place. The empty space of the stage can represent anywhere or nowhere – an inner space of imagination which exists only *in* the imagination, like the imaginary desert island on the mental stage of the radio. Fully to apprehend the significance of the settings in *The Real Thing*, it is necessary either to see or to envisage in detail the scenery for the play. The relative epistemological status of the contemporary urban interiors, exterior cityscapes and mental 'spaces' were implicitly and explicitly juxtaposed during the spectators' viewing experience. The consequent shifts from one type of visual representation to another formed a visual commentary on the levels of acting and being which the actors created in performance.

In accordance with the naturalistic principles of the well-made play which *The Real Thing* imitates and deconstructs, Stoppard makes detailed use of the naturalistic paraphernalia of setting and props to focus much of the action of the play around specific bits of stage business, making use of all the conventions of a contemporary well-made play with its doorbells to announce entrances, telephones to introduce dramatic exposition without undue contrivance of dialogue, drinks and dips being served, the radio and hi fi set to complete the illusion of a social environment and to furnish the sounds of contemporary culture.

However, the cliché appurtenances of contemporary living are not employed merely to contrive stage business that enhances the verisimilitude of scene and action; key events in the action are structured around them. Typically, the *House of Cards* foreshadows the use of such naturalistic business as turning points in the plot. On entering at the opening of the play, the architect's wife slammed the door at the moment when Jeremy Clyde warned her not to, thus causing his house of cards to collapse. Polly Adams carried '*a small suitcase and a plastic duty-free airport bag'* which contained the Alpine snowstorm souvenir. At the end of the scene, the audience had begun to realise that the witty conversation about Lake Geneva (as opposed to Virginia Water), the pronunciation of Basel (as opposed to Ba'l) and genuine Swiss watches (as opposed to Japanese digital ones) was elaborate small talk expressing in a socially acceptable manner a confrontation which might lead to the break-up of their marriage. The emotional conflict was the subtext of the scene, constituting its genuine dramatic content. In the conversation, place names were used as authenticating marks of genuine experience but they turned out to be mere alibis in the same way that the toy souvenir was a fake proof that the wife had been to Switzerland. Real proof that she had not left the country was furnished by the architect's discovery of her passport in her recipe drawer after a detailed search to ascertain whether or not she was being unfaithful.

In performance the actuality of the various props in the scene – the pyramid of cards, the sound of the doorbell, the duty-free airport bag, the suitcase, the glasses of wine poured by Jeremy Clyde, the Alpine souvenir – provided the focus for the behaviour of the actors within a precise simulacrum of social reality. These pieces of stage business served to authenticate the fictional reality of the passport, the recipe drawer, the Rembrandt place mats and the wife's lover – all mentioned but not shown on stage in the scene.

Ironically, Charlotte revealed in Scene 2 of *The Real Thing* that, in actual fact, the wife did not have a lover; her lies about the passport were a red herring thrown into the action by the playwright Henry – an implicit reminder to the audience not to apply conventional rules of interpretation to the action of what appeared to be a standard well-made play. Even such a typical example of the genre as *House of Cards* might, as in this case, contain surprise reversals which reflect a less melodramatic view of human existence than the initial situation had led the audience to expect.

In Scene 2 a more sophisticated use was made of all the typical features of such naturalistic stage business employed as blatant theatrical contrivance in *House of Cards*. At first the audience 'read' the scene with its Sunday newspapers, hi fi set and record sleeves scattered on the floor around Henry as a typical Sunday morning. Charlotte and Henry were lounging around rather aimlessly. As they talked about Henry's forthcoming appearance as a guest on *Desert Island Discs* one might have begun to notice the witty parallels between the use of place names in *House of Cards* and the various places (Deauville, Bournemouth, Zermatt) mentioned by Henry in the debonair manner of a latter-day Noel Coward as he attempted to find the name of a particular piece of waltz music by association with the holiday resort where he first heard it. This was the first introduction of the important motif of music in the play, references to music and literature (e.g. 'I was writing my Sartre play at the time' and a reference to *Finnegans Wake*) being associated with particular occasions in foreign locations. According to Henry, records chosen for *Desert Island Discs* are supposed to be associated with 'turning points in your life', once again a joking reflection on the idea that crucial moments of experience are often associated with humdrum activities or accompanied by banal pieces of popular music, great works of literature read or created in unlikely places or under trivial circumstances. This dialectic between high art and popular culture, intense emotions and cliched experiences, was precisely mirrored in the relationship between text (the trite or banal surface) and subtext (the complex, 'subterranean' reality) which constitute the conventional terms of naturalism.

Scene 2 exploited these conventions of mise-en-scène, at the same time conducting an oblique metadramatic reflection upon them. Later in the scene, sometime after the other couple, Max and Annie, have entered, a complicated social situation was orchestrated around the activities of mixing Buck's Fizz cocktails and making and serving a dip with crudités in the interstices of which Henry and Annie expressed certain intimacies, thus revealing to the audience that they were having an affair.

Another crucial turning point in the plot was engineered when Max cut his finger while opening a can of pineapple, after which Henry gave him his handkerchief to staunch the blood. Max then returned the handkerchief to Henry. In

Scene 3 it emerged that Max's discovery of Henry's blood-
and semen-stained handkerchief in Annie's car in the time
elapsing between Scenes 2 and 3 became his evidence that
Henry and Annie had been having an affair. In performance
it gradually became apparent that *The Real Thing* employed
the type of theatrical aesthetic whose clichés were illustrated
in *House of Cards*. Because the action of *The Real Thing* was
more elaborate, however, the relationship between text and
subtext appeared as more complex or oblique. As if to
remind audiences of the conventions of the genre, the climac-
tic action of *The Real Thing* consisted of a melodramatically
contrived piece of stage business, the moment when Annie
pushed the dip into Brodie's face effectively signalling her
disillusionment with Brodie's cause and at the same time
the ending of her romance with Billy. What was daring
about the effect in the theatre was that it reminded one of
the contrived climax of a well-made play at the very moment
when the action and motive of *The Real Thing* were shown
to be most complex.

One of the moments of performance most quoted in
reviews of the production was the piece of business in Scene
5 when Henry illustrated his view of art by fetching a cricket
bat from the hall and, holding it in the air, mimed the action
of batting at a dramatic point in the speech in which he
attempted to prove the necessity for sound craftsmanship as
a prerequisite for good art. This was in fact exactly the same
as the type of visual demonstration used by George on a
number of occasions in *Jumpers*. By contrast with the bow
and arrow, the different coloured left and right socks and
the tortoise and the hare, the cricket bat is a perfectly ordinary sort of object to have lying around the house. Perhaps
because of its ordinariness as an image, reviewers remembered
the conjunction of naturalistic stage business and abstract
philosophical argument as unorthodox.

At the Strand Theatre in November 1982, it appeared that
West End audiences were prepared to digest an intellectually
convoluted discourse on truth and semblance largely because
of Stoppard's brilliant exploitation of a formula with which
they were familiar. By allowing the audience the pleasure of
recognising the well-worn motifs of the West End play about

middle class adultery with its histrionic climaxes carefully
contrived around stage business conventionally used to represent familiar middle class social rituals, *The Real Thing*
managed to examine the assumptions upon which this type
of theatre (and the type of society it reflects) are based.

14   ACTING AND BEING: TEXT AND SUBTEXT

Many critics commented upon the high quality of the acting,
particularly that of Roger Rees and Felicity Kendal as Henry
and Annie, Polly Adams and Jeremy Clyde having much
less to do. A comparison with the reviews for *Jumpers* reveals
that far less detailed critical consideration was given to the
actors' performances in *The Real Thing*. The reason is that,
skilful though these were, the play called for the kind of
stock naturalistic performances which are less showy or idio-
syncratic, more obviously derived from the conventions of
naturalistic acting associated with British television drama.

The reviewers seemed in agreement that the role of Henry
offered Roger Rees better acting opportunities than the part
of Annie afforded Felicity Kendal; most noticed the way in
which the actors employed facets of their own personalities
to flesh out the characterisations:

> There is a stunning performance by Roger Rees, all nervous
> impulse and growing panic as he grabs at a telephone, claws
> at a bookcase, or simply follows Annie's departure from a
> room with hopeless resignation. Felicity Kendal's Annie also
> subtly combines impishness and passion, surrender to the
> moment and rock-fast affection. (Michael Billington, *Guardian*,
> 17 November 1982)

The acting was most effective in the moments between the
lines, Rees and Kendal registering their mutual attraction
by darting covert glances at each other during the Sunday
breakfast ritual of Scene 2; Jeremy Clyde sobbing like a

wounded animal as he clutched on to a rather expressionless Felicity Kendal at the end of Scene 3; Rees and Kendal gazing lovingly at each other after Henry's speech, 'I love love. I love having a lover and being one' at the end of Scene 5, immediately followed by the silent action of Annie (Kendal) searching through Henry's possessions a few moments after he had left the room.

A comic dialectic was established in the theatre between the reality of the actors' professional lives and the characters' fictional identities in the casting of Felicity Kendal (star of *The Good Life* and other popular television series) as the actress Annie (star of *Rosie of the Royal Infirmary*) against Roger Rees (who had just left the Royal Shakespeare Company to appear in this West End production) as the playwright Henry. The relationship between Rees' highbrow image as an intellectual actor and Kendal's pop celebrity as a kittenish TV personality was directly analogous to that of Henry the playwright and Annie the actress in *The Real Thing*. The reviews reinforce the impression that the actors created the illusion either that they *were* the characters or that the characters *were them*. This was very different to the response of the critics to Michael Hordern and Diana Rigg in *Jumpers* where what was noticed was the fact that they were *acting* with consummate skill. Just as the setting had, on one level, to be naturalistic in order for Stoppard to deconstruct its scenic conventions, so the acting had to be naturalistic in order to motivate the questions about the relationship between acting and being which are the play's central concerns.

The relationship between what the characters do and say (text) and the complexity of feeling which motivates their behaviour (subtext) is analogous to the relationship between the reality of the actors' lives and the fictional behaviour of the characters they portray. So the acting of Rees and Kendal was opaque in the sense that each created a stage persona so 'real' it was indistinguishable from the actor's personality. But because they did not play with too much fussy detail of characterisation or demonstration of motive and feeling, the audience was encouraged to fill the spaces between and beneath the lines (subtext) with the absent feelings which were implied and with which most members of the audience would freely empathise. In conjunction with the heightened rhetoric of the metadramatic scenes such refined understatement of performance, alternating with certain exceptional moments of intensely physical reaction, allowed a spectator to 'read in' the depth of feeling being repressed in the characters' external behaviour.

The other characters in the play were presented largely in terms of social behaviour. Significantly, only Max was permitted to show his passionate feelings on stage (Scene 3) and it was Max who phoned Henry at the end of the play to tell him that he (Max) was in love and about to be married again. Polly Adams was slightly arch and calculating in her performance – absolutely appropriate to her role as a strong and independent actress who despised the subservient relationships to men of the characters she was forced to play. Brodie was given a straightforward 'type' performance by Ian Oliver and Billy was played by Michael Thomas with the narcissistic attractiveness that often characterises a West End juvenile lead.

Peter Wood and his cast had realized that the trick of the playing was not to look self-consciously actorish (like Graham Crowden's Player in *Rosencrantz and Guildenstern Are Dead*) but artfully natural (like a good performance on television) so that the audience would interpret 'acting' as trendy, middle class social poise. By dissolving the boundaries between the artifice of sophisticated social behaviour and the self-awareness of contemporary naturalistic television acting, the deliberate ambiguities of *The Real Thing* were teasingly set up as a game of infinite reflections on the self-consciousness of its audience.

Just as the presence of the actors/characters enabled members of the Strand Theatre audience to imagine the characters' submerged feelings through a process of empathy, so did the moods and emotions in the music referred to in the dialogue and actually heard during scene changes, direct the audience to a perception of the simple but passionate feelings – the clichéd emotions of daily life – which for Stoppard constitute 'the real thing'. Writing in *City Limits*, Ros Asquith somewhat unwittingly captured the paradoxical quality of a play which in performance provoked one to be moved by the banal reality of romantic passion by means of a theatrical process which rendered its own form invisible: 'I found my happiest moments were spent listening to the Golden Oldies which punctuated the scenes. Could the whole exercise be a subtle Stoppardian joke intended to prove that the Righteous Brothers really could say more about love in two minutes than the playwright can in two hours?' (24 November 1982). To have answered yes would have been to perceive how consistent and how modern is Stoppard's view of the confrontation between high culture and popular art.

READING LIST

Texts

The first edition of each of the plays has been subject to minor revision by the playwright to reflect changes made in the light of the first or subsequent productions; *The Real Thing* has been reprinted in two slightly different versions. In all cases, quotations are from the most recently revised text.

Background and Criticism

Michael Billington, *Stoppard the Playwright* (Methuen, London and New York, 1987), is a lively and opinionated introduction to the original plays and adaptations written before 1986, which recognises with approval evidence of a growing political and social commitment in the plays written after 1976. It includes a brief discussion of each of the three plays examined in this volume.

Tim Brassell, *Tom Stoppard: An Assessment* (Macmillan, London 1985), presents a careful and detailed analysis of the intellectual coherence of Stoppard's drama with individual chapters on *Rosencrantz and Guildenstern Are Dead* and *Jumpers*.

C. W. E. Bigsby, *Tom Stoppard* (Longmans, London, 1976; enlarged edition, 1979), is a pithy introduction to the themes and structure of the earlier plays.

Ronald Hayman, *Tom Stoppard* (Heinemann, London, 1977); enlarged edition, gives a concise account of the earlier plays with individual chapters on *Rosencrantz and Guildenstern Are Dead* and *Jumpers*. It contains two interviews with Stoppard.

Anthony Jenkins, *The Theatre of Tom Stoppard* (Cambridge

University Press, Cambridge, 1987; revised edition 1989), includes a balanced interpretation of each of the three plays and provides the most up-to-date account of Stoppard's most recent theatre work.

Malcolm Page, *File on Stoppard* (Methuen, London, 1986), is a useful compilation of extracts from interviews, reviews and information on the playwright and his work.

Kenneth Tynan, *Show People* (Weidenfeld & Nicolson, London, 1980), contains a stimulating and witty appreciation of Stoppard's early work, including *Rosencrantz and Guildenstern Are Dead* and *Jumpers*.

Thomas R. Whitaker, *Tom Stoppard* (Macmillan, Modern Dramatists series, London, 1983), contains a chapter each on *Rosencrantz and Guildenstern Are Dead* and *Jumpers*, emphasising the aesthetics of play which underlies the theatrical structure of Stoppard's work.

INDEX OF NAMES